Fast Walking

RON LAIRD

Fast Walking

R O N   L A I R D

STACKPOLE
BOOKS

Published by
STACKPOLE BOOKS
5067 Ritter Road
Mechanicsburg, PA 17055
www.stackpolebooks.com

Printed in United States

10 9 8 7 6 5 4 3 2 1

First edition

Cover photo of Beverly LaVeck (left) and Julie Swann by Ida Brown.
Cover design by Sage Advice Ltd.

Library of Congress Cataloging-in-Publication Data
Laird, Ron, 1938–
        Fast walking/Ron Laird.—1st ed.
              p.   cm.
        Includes bibliographic references.
        ISBN 0-8117-2758-0 (pbk.)
        1. Walking (Sports)   I. Title.
        GV1071 .L35 2000
        796.51—dc21

                                                                    00-029702

Contents

Ashtabula, Ohio, June 1996. The author race walks the Olympic torch to the Games in Atlanta.

Introduction

Everyone agrees that walking is good for you; why not learn how to walk faster and then add it to your health-care program? Even if you've had trouble learning other sports, I'm sure you can master this one and look good doing it.

Fast walking is an excellent way to burn calories and lose weight. When practiced regularly, it will trim and tone flabby areas and restore elasticity, strength, and endurance to your muscles, heart, and lungs. It's an activity for all ages and abilities, and can be practiced just about anywhere. It's one of the most practical forms of exercise.

Walking is an inexpensive activity. You don't need to buy special clothes; anything loose and comfortable will do, although you should always invest in quality shoes, as you don't want to risk a foot or leg injury.

There's no need to join some sort of club, and you don't have to depend on partners, opponents, or trainers to get you through an exercise session. By walking alone, you can concentrate more on what you're doing, and go where you wish and at the pace you prefer.

Fast walking is not hard to learn. Because of its low impact on your entire body, it is quite safe to walk at a quick pace. The unique hip, knee, and arm action of fast walking allows you to move your legs quickly and efficiently. There is little pounding to hurt your feet and the joints of your legs, hips, and back. Your body was designed for walking.

At first your mind and body may do some rebelling against this different way of walking. There will be times when workouts go poorly and motivation is low. If you bear with a consistent training program for a couple of months, your improvements will make all your effort

The author finishes a 20-km race in the Los Angeles Coliseum in the summer of 1967.

It's heel and toe and away they go! Walkers of all ages start off to meet the challenges of a race.

seem well worth it. As you see and feel yourself getting fitter, your desire to keep at it will grow. The right type of walking improves health, posture, coordination, and self-confidence, and you can enjoy the benefits of fast walking throughout your lifetime.

Your first goal will be to master correct fast-walking technique. Speed will come once you've learned and practiced correct style for a while. The technique you'll be learning from these pages is that used by other fast walkers all over the world.

The desire to take part in organized races is often of little interest to beginners. But as time goes by and improvements are seen and felt, most change their minds. As their confidence and ability grow, they find themselves on the starting line of short races just out of curiosity or for the fun or challenge of it.

Racing opportunities can be found in track meets, road races, and in special walk divisions of road-running events. Most are at distances of

1 mile to 5 kilometers (3.1 miles) in track meets, and 5 to 10 kilometers and beyond on the roads. For those drawn to longer contests, there are quite a few marathons (26.2 miles) and half marathons with walking divisions in which to test your technique, training, and courage. Fifty-kilometer (31.1-mile) race walks are hard to find. Even though this event has the distinction of being the longest foot race in the Olympic Games, few individuals have the desire to train and compete in it. This race has to be one of the toughest athletic contests ever invented, but perhaps the 50-kilometer is the sort of challenge you've been looking for. Men also race the shorter, 20-kilometer (12.4-mile) event in the Olympic Games, world championships, and other major international contests. The standard distance for women race walkers in these same competitions is now 20 kilometers.

In order to stress the endurance characteristic of competitive walking and to judge it more accurately, the women's 10-kilometer was doubled to

A fast walker and two runners go at it in a 10-km mixed (runners and walkers) race near Seattle. These two disciplines coexist nicely on the roads of the world.

20 kilometers two years before the 2000 Olympics in Sydney, Australia. To qualify for various U.S. national teams, race walkers must always place near the front in a selection race and often meet very strict time standards.

I first got into this fitness and competitive activity back in 1955 when I was seventeen years old. I competed in nearly thirty tryout races throughout my young, serious years and never could keep from suffering the nervousness they created, especially when I had a chance to do well. But such emotions, if controlled, can help your performance by causing you to move faster while feeling the effort less. Talk yourself into looking forward to the onset and buildup of such anxieties. The more of those juices flowing through your bloodstream, the harder, faster, and longer you'll be able to push yourself.

My first experience with competitive walking was a 2-mile track race in the Bronx, New York, in July 1955. Back then my interest was in distance running and discus and javelin throwing.

Plattsburgh, New York, 1976. Olympians (from left) Todd Scully, Ron Laird, and Larry Walker give President Ford a quick lesson in the art of fast walking. The president came to give our track and field team a pep talk just before we left for the Montreal Games.

In most races, men and women compete together but in separate age and gender categories.

The walk was the last event on the program that evening. I entered it out of curiosity and the desire for some more physical activity. I had only a few minutes to learn the basics of how to do it by watching some others as they warmed up. By copying and trying what I saw them doing, I quickly learned the fundamentals of this Olympic event. My technique was correct, but the race turned out to be a rough experience, because I tried to go too fast. My leg muscles really rebelled. They had been trained differently from two years of high-school running.

Even though I finished last in that 2-mile contest, I took an interest in the event and decided to stick with it for the rest of my summer vacation. At the end of those weeks, I liked race walking so much that I abandoned the running and weight-throwing events. The encouragement of new friends and the chance to compete in such a unique event helped get me addicted.

During my first dozen or so years of racing, I tried to take part in everything that came along, from 1 mile to 50 kilometers. Weekend races always motivated me to train well throughout the rest of the week. Living in the New York City area gave me plenty of opportunities at both indoor and outdoor events. If there weren't any walks between Boston and Washington that weekend, I'd enter a local road run and race walk it to get a long, hard workout. Even though some race organizers back then tried to discourage me, I still paid my entry fee and took off with all the runners. It was always important for me to achieve a strong training session. Fighting it out with slower runners who didn't like being beaten by a walker made all of us work harder. Today many road runs include a race-walking and/or strolling division. If they don't, you can always enter the road run anyway just to get a good workout and to see if you can beat any of the slower runners.

If you don't attempt to walk faster and farther than your physical condition allows, races can be entertaining. If you never try your legs at racing, that's okay. The health and well-being you achieve are the most important benefits. Your fitness activities should always be designed to promote your quality of life.

Whether you get high-quality exercise from walking depends on how fast and how far you walk. To improve your fitness, you need to fast walk 70 to 80 percent of your maximum heart rate. With the correct fast-walking technique and enough effort, you'll get all the exercise your mind and body need. There will always be an opportunity to improve and thus achieve more than you first thought possible. Those who train seriously are usually surprised at their rapid improvement after a few months.

Because of fast walking's smooth, low-impact contact and flow over the ground, there is little chance of joint-jarring injuries. Correct technique allows you to move safely at a fast pace over distances that are long enough to really benefit your mind and body. What better hobby is there than one that improves your health?

Think of fast walking as the missing link between ordinary walking and running. As a beginner, you should progress from ordinary walking to fast walking at various speeds and distances before going on to running, and along the way, you may enjoy fast walking so much that you never make it into the running game. If you put the time and work into it, the exercise you get from fast walking can equal or even surpass what you get from running. Plus, it's much easier on your feet, legs, and lower back.

As with such sports as bowling, skating, cycling, golf, and swimming, your proficiency at fast walking will take time and effort to develop. This form of walking is likely to feel odd at first, but it will feel more natural as you consistently get out there and practice. Don't give up. Give it an honest try for at least three to six months. By then, you'll notice that your health has improved. You'll also appreciate the safety of this low-impact activity after you have practiced it for a while. The time will come when you'll be glad you stuck it out.

Always try to use good style, no matter what speed or distance you attempt. Concentrate on what you're doing if you wish to do it well. I could never rely on natural ability, because I had very little of it. Sticking to my goals, plus lots of work, eventually brought me success.

Go slowly and make sure you master correct style first. Have faith in yourself and in what your workouts will do for you. Perseverance is a must if you are to eventually realize your fitness goals.

Take good care of your health. No one else is going to do it for you. You are responsible for your lifestyle. Only you can do the required exercise and eat the right foods that will make good health possible. Be at war with the desires to overeat and be lazy. Make time for yourself to take a walk and exercise. To be healthy, you would be wise to devote at least forty minutes to an hour per day. Make your walks provide you with beneficial exercise and enjoyment.

The best way to get fit and lose fat is with a combination of aerobic exercise, strength training, and a healthy, low-fat diet. Since low-impact, endurance-type exercise is best, walking at various speeds and distances can form an excellent and inexpensive health-care program. Use your fast walking to prolong and enhance your life. If you are a happier person, others will enjoy being around you more. It's hard to feel bad about

The start of a walking race in southern California. Millions of people use walking as their main fitness activity. More should try race walking before rushing into running, which is more injury-prone.

yourself if you put the effort into what it takes to look and feel good. You're never too old to get positive results.

Combine your fast walking with enough sleep and nutrition, and you'll be on your way to a happier and healthier life. Give it a fair try. I hope that one of these days you'll be as convinced as I am that it's better to walk fast than to run slow.

The information in the following pages will teach you how to walk fast and safely enough to vigorously exercise all the muscles of your body, plus your respiratory and circulatory systems. Everything here is meant to explain and illustrate how to walk your fastest and do it within the rules of the sport. You'll learn the rules and basic technique used by world-class men and women race walkers around the world. The judging chapter also describes ways to improve your legality.

Best of health and success!

Getting 1 Started

CORRECT TECHNIQUE

Correct fast-walking technique will move you along with an efficient, continuous flow. Contrast this with your common street form of walking, which is a series of steps with a slight up-and-down action. Switching back and forth a few times for a dozen steps of each style will quickly convince you of the difference in fluency.

Stay smooth. Glide along and enjoy yourself. Think about how you are moving, regardless of pace. Concentrate and work on the different parts of the fast-walk movement to perfect them. I often practice doing this during workouts and races, and even when I'm just walking at a slow pace. Overdoing arm, hip, leg, and foot work during various training drills will make you stronger and more flexible. Strength and flexibility will always improve your technique, endurance, and speed.

It's important to achieve and maintain proper body balance at all times. Keep an upright posture with your hips directly underneath you. Whether fast walking on level ground, uphill, or down, maintain a posture that will constantly improve your forward progression and help keep you legal. Don't let fatigue and loss of concentration cause you to lean back to where you are fighting your body weight and forward momentum.

Walking at a quick pace while dealing with fatigue takes a lot of concentration and exertion. The more attention you pay to your technique, balance, and effort, the better and longer you'll be able to walk. Your perseverance will be rewarded.

Take care not to slightly twist your body to one side as you walk. This could be a burden to balance, posture, and momentum and might cause discomfort if overdone. Try not to give in to an urge to walk fast by bending at the waist and

leaning way forward, lowering and pumping your arms, and taking extralong steps. Leaning too far forward from your ankles or waist puts extra pressure on the knee joint of your lead leg as your body weight drops down onto its heel. The discomfort this causes could encourage you to start landing on a bent knee and to lose some or all of your hip rolling and turning action. Pressing your hips forward a little will help straighten you up. Keep your upper body directly on top of your hips. Good posture aids forward momentum and makes you look good.

People often use the hiking style of walking fast because it feels so natural, but its mechanics make it inefficient, slow, and tiring when compared with the efficiency and leg speed of correct fast walking. Nevertheless, the hiking style is the safest way of walking up and down very steep inclines and rough and slippery surfaces.

A prancing style will help you turn your legs over quicker, but it's dangerous because it can easily bounce you up and off the ground. In races, it catches the attention of judges because it can look like a jogging motion if done poorly.

Correct technique, with its emphasis on hip turning, helps the high-speed walker maintain better contact with the ground. If done with good effort, your muscles, heart, and lungs always get an effective workout. Be aware of how you are moving so that you can try to eliminate wasted motions that would cause fatigue and slow you down.

Hip Movement

The classic hip roll is the first thing to learn. Combine it with knee straightening and 90-degree arm pumping, and you've mastered the basics of fast walking.

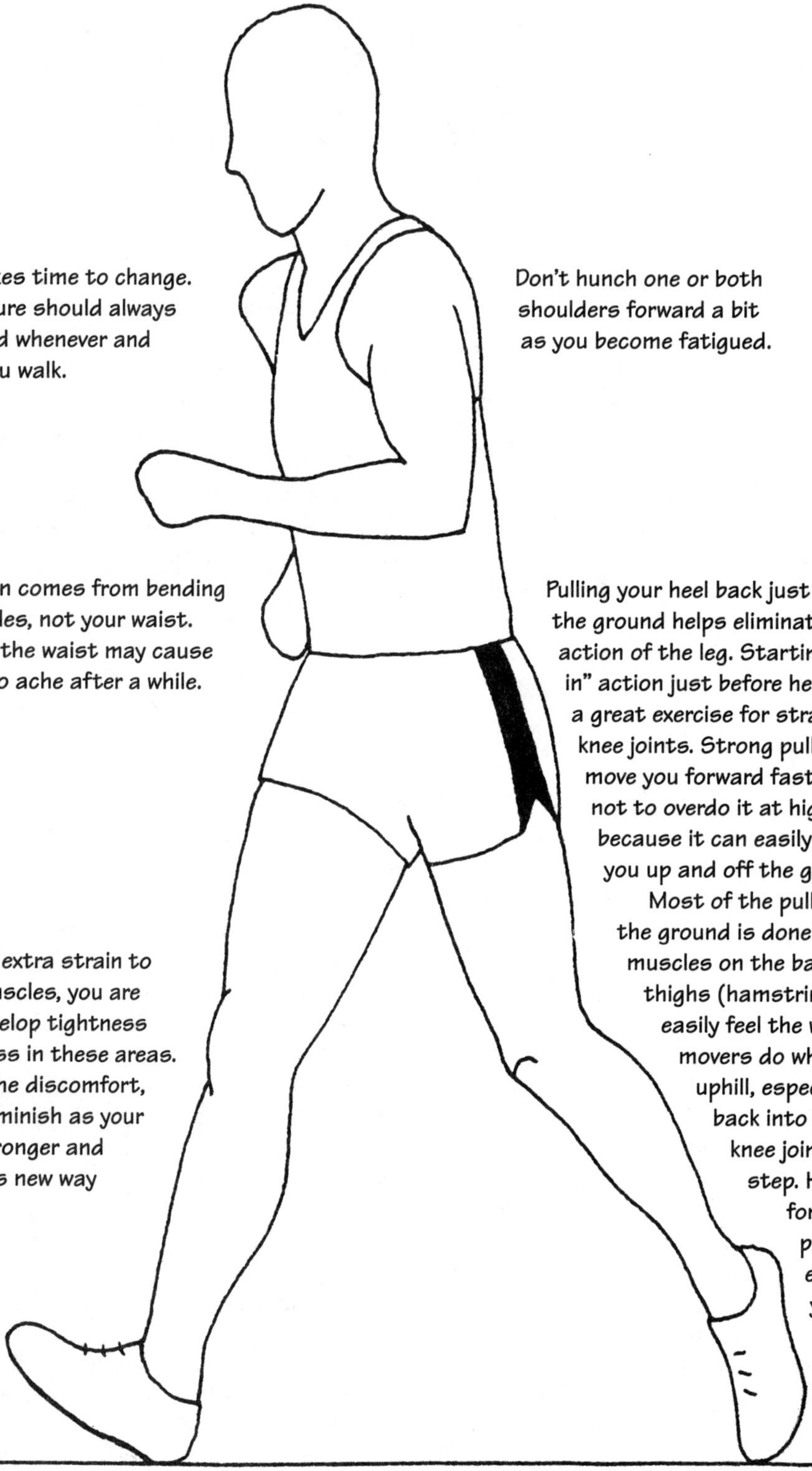

Posture takes time to change.
Good posture should always
be practiced whenever and
wherever you walk.

Don't hunch one or both
shoulders forward a bit
as you become fatigued.

Forward lean comes from bending
at your ankles, not your waist.
Bending at the waist may cause
your back to ache after a while.

Pulling your heel back just as it contacts
the ground helps eliminate the breaking
action of the leg. Starting this "digging
in" action just before heel strike is also
a great exercise for straightening out
knee joints. Strong pulling always helps
move you forward faster. Be careful
not to overdo it at high speeds
because it can easily bounce
you up and off the ground.

Most of the pulling back of
the ground is done with the large
muscles on the backs of your
thighs (hamstrings). You can
easily feel the work these prime
movers do when race walking
uphill, especially if you sit
back into your hip and
knee joints with each
step. Hill work is great
for building the
pulling power and
endurance of
your hamstrings.

Because of extra strain to
the shin muscles, you are
likely to develop tightness
and soreness in these areas.
Bear with the discomfort,
for it will diminish as your
legs get stronger and
used to this new way
of walking.

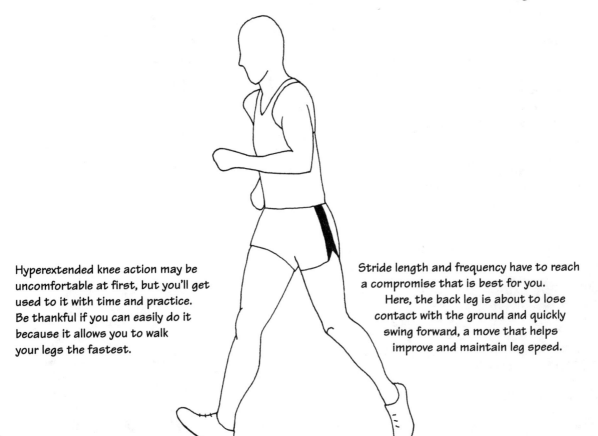

Hyperextended knee action may be uncomfortable at first, but you'll get used to it with time and practice. Be thankful if you can easily do it because it allows you to walk your legs the fastest.

Stride length and frequency have to reach a compromise that is best for you. Here, the back leg is about to lose contact with the ground and quickly swing forward, a move that helps improve and maintain leg speed.

Hip rolling lets you walk your fastest. When it's combined with front-to-rear hip turning, you achieve a longer stride. Even though it's natural for hip turning to cause the entire supporting leg and foot to twist inward a bit as it moves behind you, try to avoid overdoing it, or it will soon tire you out and slow you down. Flexibility exercises for hips, stomach, and lower back will help reduce the potentially harmful effects of too much leg torquing.

Hip rolling and turning need to be just right for each individual and the walking situations encountered. To get a feeling of how this looks and works, follow the back-and-forth movement of the stripe on the side of the shorts in the drawings throughout this book.

The motion of your hips must be uninhibited, because they perform the most important part of the fast-walking movement. Their rolling, drop-ping, and twisting action makes it possible to move your legs quickly and efficiently. You must master this unique hip motion in order to walk your fastest. Hip and lower-back flexibility is also very important. Good flexibility and hip turning improve stride length and help you hold better ground contact during fast walking.

All the rolling and turning action helps tone the muscles of your mid-section.

Leg Straightening

To walk your fastest, and to satisfy the judges, your knee joint needs to be straight, or as far back as it can go, when your heel contacts the ground. Your knee is *not* allowed to be slightly bent when it lands. Once your leg has landed, it must stay straight until it is directly underneath you before it may be bent.

This action photo shows the author twisting back into his hip joint in an effort to keep both feet from coming off the ground at the same time during high-speed race walking. Sitting back into the hip and knee joint does help to hold the rear foot down on the ground an instant longer. If done well, good hip action will also help thrust your body forward and lengthen your stride a bit. You will need to work on the continual concentration, flexibility, and effort that it requires. Lower-back and stomach muscles do get plenty of exercise during good back-and-forth hip turning.

Here, the author uses hip turning to get by the judges and walk a mile in 6 minutes and 22 seconds. The event took place in Madison Square Garden in February 1968, on a 160-yard (11 laps to the mile) track made of rubber-covered sheets of plywood. This surface provided very good traction but was a bit bouncy in places.

Make sure the hips work in a straight front-to-rear and rear-to-front motion. Excessive hip action off to either side will be wasteful, tiring, and unsightly.

Early knee straightening and hip rolling are musts for quick leg turnover. The working together of these two functions is what makes you a true fast walker. Master them and you'll be on your way to walking with the same style used by Olympians all over the world.

The ability to easily and naturally hyperextend, or brace back, the knee joint definitely comes in handy when you want to walk fast. I know of no other athletic event that can claim this unique leg movement. Other sports require you to bend your knees and use the large muscles on the fronts of your thighs to do most of the work of thrusting you straight ahead, into the air, or off into different directions. Fast walking's straight-knee action makes you use hip rotation and the muscles on the backs of your thighs to do most of the work of moving you forward.

Head Position

Keep your head up and facing forward. Don't let your chin drop down toward your chest. As your mouth opens to take in more air, keep jaw, face, and neck muscles relaxed. These muscles may be the first to tense up during times of stress. Stay aware of what they are doing so you can keep them under control.

Arm Pumping

The arms are moved as in regular walking, swinging counter to the legs. Hold the elbows at 90-degree angles and pump them vigorously. Their angle should close a bit when going fast and open a little more than 90 degrees when moving at a slower pace. Let them come across your chest in a pattern most comfortable for your body structure. When an arm comes across the chest, it helps bring the opposite hip around, thus increasing your stride length a little. Swinging your arms straight back and forth in a motion that is parallel to the sides of your body can restrict the natural and beneficial front-to-rear turning of your hips. Although runners benefit from a straighter back-and-forth arm movement, fast walkers need to pump their arms across their chests more to aid their front-to-rear hip turning. Swinging the arms across the chest makes it easier for the hips to twist back and forth and extend the stride. Driving the elbows back and up gives good lift and tone to the chest muscles.

The faster you move your legs, the faster and more economical your arm pumping must be. A shorter and quicker arm swing will always help speed you up. If you're going to walk at a slower pace, hold your arms lower and swing them easier.

The hip rolling and dropping, straight-knee action, and vigorous arm pumping should feel different at first. As you gradually get used to these movements, they'll make more sense to you because of the speed at which they allow you to move your legs. The more you practice this new form of exercise, the more comfortable you'll feel with it and the better you'll like it.

Foot Placement

Hip rolling and leg straightening will be easier to do once you've mastered proper foot placement. They work together to make you move and look your best.

Some pain in the back of the knees is normal for beginners. It will diminish as the tendons and muscles get stretched and used to this quick way of walking. Low knee action helps you maintain proper contact with the ground.

Glance down to see if your feet are landing with toes pointed straight ahead. A good way to check their alignment is to walk through a puddle of water, and then loop around to look at your footprints before they dry.

Push straight forward with the toes and ankles. Try not to twist your heel inward as your back foot comes up on its toes. Vigorous ankle and toe pushing helps keep your speed and momentum going.

Hip flexibility helps reduce most of the inward twisting of the heels as the toes push off. If the heel torques inward too much, the leg will be in a slightly twisted position as it comes forward. This could eventually cause strain to hip and hamstring areas.

Hip flexibility and turning bring your feet into proper alignment. Pumping your arms across your chest also helps bring your hips around so that your feet end up where they belong.

It's good practice to place your body weight slightly to the outside of your foot and leg as you fast walk. This helps you achieve a little better hip rolling and leg speed. Foot doctors have told me that rolling along the outside of the foot is the most stable way for the feet to land. Don't push your hip out to your side as it comes in underneath you; that move would be a waste of energy. Avoid landing and rolling to the inside of your foot. This is likely to cause pain and even injury if done long enough.

If you have heavy thighs, correct foot placement will be more difficult. As you lose weight, it

When walking at a slow place, hold your hands lower. When moving faster, bring them up to the classic 90-degree bend at the elbow.

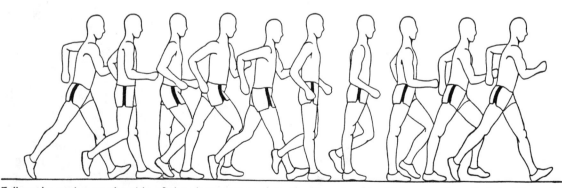

Follow the stripe on the side of the shorts to see how the hips should roll/drop and turn/twist with each step. Correct knee straightening and arm action are also illustrated.

May 1964, Mt. San Antonio College, Walnut, Calif. Continual effort and concentration helped me set fourteen American records at distances of 6 kms to 10 miles. My hips did a lot of quick wiggling all during that late afternoon effort of 1 hour, 13 minutes, and 17.6 seconds.

Don't let the expression on my face alarm you. I was quite fit and didn't feel as bad as I look.

Hands swing close to hips as they move back and forth. They need not come up in front any higher than breast level. Don't let your hands flop around at the wrists.

A slight turning of your ankle to the outside just before your foot lands will help place you on the outside edge of your heel and keep you to the outside of your shin, knee, thigh, and hip as they pass underneath and behind you. This is the healthiest way for your feet to land, and it also helps you master and maintain correct hip rolling.

You don't have to walk on that outer edge all the time, especially if you're going slowly. Switch back and forth now and then as you move along. As with everything in technique and training, don't overdo it.

Rear view of hip drop and thrusting back action into hip and knee joint.

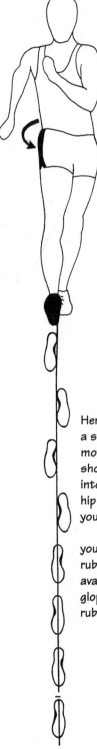

When your arms come across your chest they help rotate your hips back and forth. Hip turning causes you to have better contact with the ground. Arm movement is a big aid in controlling stride rate and length, and body balance.

Walk on a straight line with your feet landing directly in front of you. On either side of the line or down the middle is fine.

This is not the way your feet should land. Splayed-out steps are inefficient, look bad, and slow you down.

Here, the feet are landing on a straight line. The hip-turning motion (see stripe on side of shorts) helps bring leg and foot into correct alignment. Quick hip and arm action makes your legs move faster.

Before the bottoms of your shoes start to show wear, rub on a few coats of Shoe-Goo, available at shoe stores. This glop dries to form a hard, rubbery coating.

These steps are too widely spaced. They waste energy and slow you down by making your body weave from side to side. Wide steps may even cause your back to ache after a while.

Race walking to the outside of your foot and leg aids hip rolling and leg speed.

will be easier to place your feet along or on top of a straight line. To help eliminate chafing, use a skin lubricant such as Vaseline between legs and under arms.

Foot and Leg Movement

By using your ankle and shin muscles to force your toes up an instant longer after your heel touches, you help rock yourself forward along the bottom of your foot with less break to forward momentum. Try this for 50 yards to see if you can feel it slightly improving your speed and forward lean. Flexing the ankle upward just before your heel contacts the ground will also help lengthen your stride a bit. These moves develop shin and ankle strength, and will help prevent sprained ankles in whatever you do. If your ankles and

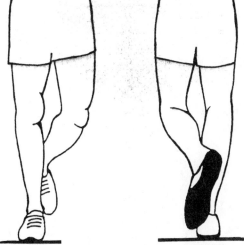

Try not to let your heels twist too much to the inside with each step, as shown. The torquing strain this sends up through the legs may cause pain and even injury. This inefficient twisting is also tiring and will wear out the bottoms of your shoes faster. Bring the leg and foot straight forward. This uneconomic movement caused me to suffer much pain and injury from the mid-1960s to early 1970s. I did it to help me stay more legal by keeping my hind foot on the ground an instant longer during high-speed race walking. I should have been wise enough to realize the problems this might cause and eliminated a lot of that harmful twisting from the way I was walking.

shins are weak, your feet will soon be flopping to the ground just after your heels hit.

Whipping your hind leg quickly forward is a good way to help improve leg speed. Try not to snap your hind foot off the ground the instant before the heel of your forward-stepping foot has time to make contact. Light (2- to 5-lb.) ankle weights help build quickness and stamina in this move. Rapid hip turning also helps you bring the trailing leg quickly forward. Be sure to keep feet and knees low at all times.

Stride

Your first fast-walking steps should feel a bit shorter but noticeably quicker and smoother. Once you get moving and well warmed up, your stride length will increase a little; as fatigue sets in, it shortens a bit.

Take steps that are normal and comfortable for your body structure and its present level of fitness. Let your speed come from how fast you move your legs. Your stride length will take care of itself as you become fitter and more flexible in the hips and lower back. Trying to reach out too far with each stride while moving quickly is fatiguing and can easily float you up and off the ground enough

to be detected by competent judges. However, overstriding while fast walking a little more slowly is very good exercise.

Running allows you to achieve a long stride, as you fly up and over the ground during each step. The unique movement of fast walking lets you move your legs just as fast as a runner but keeps your stride short by holding your feet on, or very close to, the ground.

Learning Proper Style

It's normal for beginners to wonder if they're doing everything correctly. Watching your shadow is a quick and fairly accurate way of examining your fast-walking technique. With the sun angled from behind you, check to see if one of your shoulders is rising higher than the other as you move at various speeds. If this is happening, it could mean that your waist is slightly twisted to the opposite side of that rising shoulder, the arm of that shoulder is swinging more across your chest, or both. Any wasted hip motion off to your sides can also be detected and corrected when you view your shadow with the sun directly behind you.

As you fast walk with the sun at your side, you can look at your shadow to see how well your

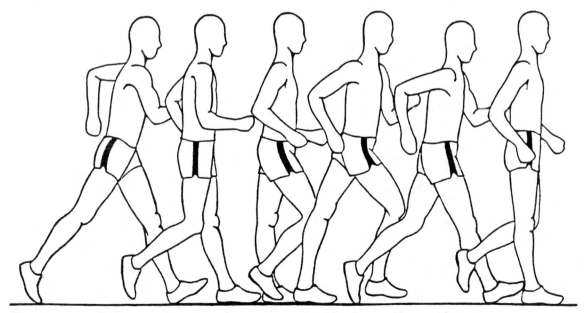

Give your steps the power and leverage of your arms, waist, hips, legs, ankles, and feet.

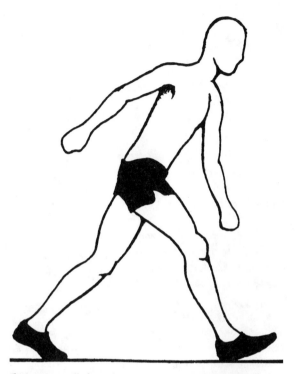

The lower back is arched too much. This shortens stride, retards proper hip action, strains the lower back, and really looks bad. Use good posture and hip action to exercise and strengthen your lower back. Never pinch your shoulder blades together.

Trying to walk fast by using too long a stride, too much forward lean, and too low an arm swing is uneconomical. This action causes much of the hip-rolling, knee-straightening, and arm-pumping efficiency of fast walking to be eliminated and turns you into a power walker. Power walking is a grand form of exercise, but it is not the racing style used in the Olympics. You can experience the contrast in quickness and effort by moving from one to the other.

After studying and practicing the competitive style of walking, you may decide to use a hiking style for most of your walks. Whenever you wish to give your muscles, heart, and lungs more exercise, switch over to the quicker technique of fast walking and use it to move faster.

Sometimes I see people trying to fast walk while only using proper arm action. From the waist down, they use a hiking style. If the arms are to be bent and pumped at the classic 90-degree angle, proper hip and knee action also need to be used to correctly complete the movement. Fast walking above the waist while trudging below the waist looks odd and restricts leg speed and efficiency.

Since breathing is a natural function that pretty much takes care of itself, you should not have to think about it. However, do experiment with different breathing patterns to see how they make you feel and perform.

Keep shoulder and arm movement controlled. Don't let your shoulders hunch upward with each forward and backward arm swing. Keep them level. Dropping the shoulder slightly downward with each forward arm swing helps you stay on the ground during high-speed walking.

Help push yourself forward by vigorously dropping or sitting back into your hips with each step. As you roll back into them, they help move your legs quicker and make your walking a series of low-impact steps.

Landing on a slightly bent knee and using it to drive you forward as you quickly straighten it out underneath and behind you is a bit tricky, but why bother? The rules say that your knee must be straight as your heel touches the ground. If it isn't, you will get into trouble with the judges. Bent knees are very easy to spot.

Feel the thrust and stability along the outside of your legs as you pull back into your knees and hips with each step.

This photo illustrates good hip drop, knee bracing, and relaxed frontal thigh muscles of the supporting leg.

Never hold your stomach in. This causes you to slow down a bit by obstructing your oxygen intake.

The muscles on the fronts of both thighs should stay relaxed. The straight-knee action of race walking offers rest to those who overuse these large muscles. Keep knees and feet close to the ground as you quickly swing them forward. Any sort of a prancing action along with too high a knee swing will cause loss of contact when moving fast. Competent judges will detect this lifting action if it is overdone, and move to disqualify you.

The braced-back position of the knee may look painful, but have no worry. The knee joint is built to take it. You should feel some stretching and pain in the backs of the knees until the muscles and tendons get used to their new way of working.

Lean forward from your ankles, but don't overdo it.

legs are straightening, whether your lower back has too much sway, and that your head isn't leaning too far forward. Shadow watching lets you see and then feel the changes you make as soon as you make them. You can also use reflections from large glass windows and doors, but these don't give you much time to study your style. An ideal situation would be to walk on a treadmill with full-length mirrors at your front and sides. Also consider having someone videotape you.

Keep reviewing the information throughout this book, and try to copy what's demonstrated on these pages. The photos, illustrations, and text will give you a good idea of how you should look and feel. Once you know what an improvement to your technique feels like, remember it and practice it until it's a permanent part of your workouts and races.

If your fast walking feels strange but your legs are moving quicker and smoother, with less pounding, you're probably doing it right. Don't try to master some sort of bent-knee shuffle because it feels fast and easy. Faultless style and healthful walks should always be your goals.

It's not always best to copy someone else's way of fast walking exactly. What works well for others may not work so well for you. Because our skeletal and muscular systems are all a little different, we need to perfect a style that is the most comfortable and natural for our own bodies. Over the years I've seen all sizes and shapes do the work needed to become accomplished race walkers. Some have even become champions. What counts is finding those small variations of basic technique that work best for you.

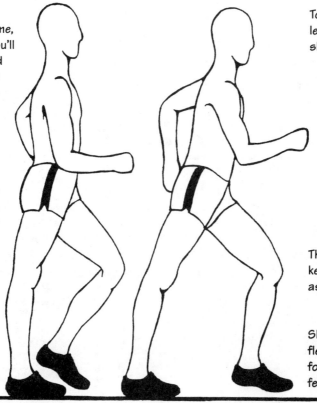

After practicing proper technique for a short time, there's a good chance you'll feel some stretching and soreness in the tendons on the back of your knee joints and the shin muscles on the front of your lower legs. The hips should feel fine as you sit back into them with each step. They act like big shock absorbers, allowing you to progress in a series of low-impact steps.

Gentle steps make it safe for you to always enjoy the stability and efficiency of walking on hard surfaces like concrete and asphalt.

Too much forward head lean strains neck and shoulder muscles.

The knee and foot are kept close to the ground as they come forward.

Slenderness and flexibility make it easier for you to place your feet on a straight line.

Keep your head up and facing straight forward.

The hip roll moves your legs fast. The hip turn increases your stride. Both are great exercise and help build muscle and burn fat.

The figure shows excellent double contact. The heel and toe areas of the shoes are on the ground at the same instant.

Fast walking's unique, low-impact heel-and-toe action is kind to your Achilles tendons. The upward pointing of the toes upon landing gently stretches them with each step. Since most of your body weight is so far forward at the end of each stride, the Achilles tendons don't get much strain at pushoff. With all the pounding and strain to legs and feet that runners endure, it's no wonder they have so many Achilles tendon and knee problems.

Always try to maintain a body balance that will assist your forward progression. This is especially important when you try to walk fast or far.

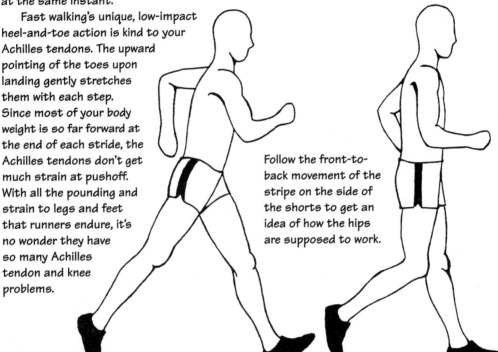

Follow the front-to-back movement of the stripe on the side of the shorts to get an idea of how the hips are supposed to work.

Foot and ankle action is used to help control the smoothness and glide of the steps.

A low back kick saves energy and looks good to the judges.

Pulling your heel back at or just before contact helps you maintain momentum and thrusts your body forward.

The knee doesn't need to be as hyperextended as shown, but it does need to be straight the instant your heel touches the ground. Sitting back into the hip and knee joints after the heel hits creates the classic fast-walking style, efficiency, and speed. It's good if your knees are able to flop easily and automatically back into their joints. This action will help you to move your legs efficiently and quickly.

If you open the angle of your arms and swing them in a longer arc out across your chest and behind you, you'll also help lengthen your stride. If you overdo your arm action, you waste energy and slow your leg speed. When you close your arms a little less than 90 degrees and pump them closer to your body, you help your legs move their fastest. During this quick arm pumping, you should restrict your backswing a bit by not letting your hands drive back any farther than your hips.

No matter how tired you get, do not tighten your shoulder blades together.

Lean forward from your ankles, not your waist. Use your ankles to help you stay more to the outside of your feet and legs. Your legs and feet are strong and stable along their outside edges. Rolling along on the outside of your feet and legs helps you fast walk your quickest because it promotes correct hip action and efficiency.

Your arms are held at about 90 degrees and pumped vigorously.

Because of hip drop, the forward-swinging foot just clears the ground. Don't let your hips sway off to your sides. Keep them pivoting back and forth, as if they were on an axis running straight down through the center of your body. Keep your chin up. An upright trunk promotes good hip movement and legal knee action. Thrusting back into your hip while still pulling back with the same leg will push the body forward and help swing the opposite leg through.

It's harder to walk fast in clumsy shoes. Use lightweight shoes that complement your high-speed coordination and effort.

When not sight-seeing, look 40 to 50 yards ahead of where you're walking. Glance down frequently to be sure the surface is clear of obstructions.

Don't throw your arms off to your sides as you swing them behind you. Your hands should just clear your sides as they move back and forth.

Maintaining proper technique, breathing, balance, and effort will give you plenty to think about.

Don't let your hands and wrists flop around. At different speeds, they move naturally to aid your balance.

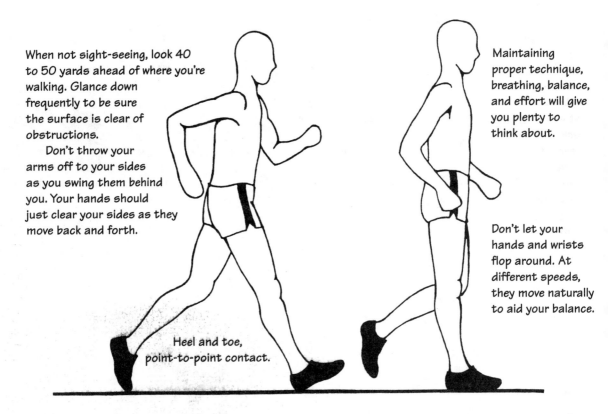

Heel and toe, point-to-point contact.

Pulling and pushing the ground back along the outside of your foot, leg, and hip provides the best alignment for maximum speed and power.

Keeping the trail leg low is economical, makes for good contact, and pleases the judges. Try to do this without twisting your heels to the inside. Bring your foot and leg straight forward.

The slower you walk, the lower you should swing your hands. If you bring your arms up into the classic 90-degree fast-walking position, combine it with proper hip and knee action and some speed. You'll look better and get more exercise if you do.

So that you can move properly, you need flexibility in your hips and lower back. Use fast walking and specific exercises to loosen, stretch, and strengthen these areas.

Have confidence in what you're doing. Set realistic goals and have patience.

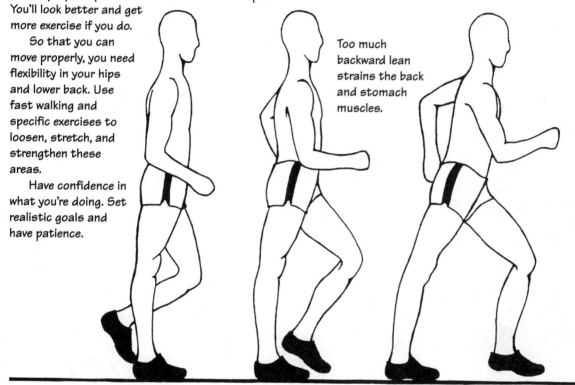

Too much backward lean strains the back and stomach muscles.

It will take time and effort to build up and strengthen your shins.

Rough surfaces, small stones, and twigs can cause you to twist your foot and ankle under you as you roll along the outside edge. Stay alert to what you're stepping on.

After pulling yourself forward with your hamstring muscles, keep pushing yourself forward with calves, ankles, balls of feet, and toes.

You always need to put good effort into your arm swing. Even if your legs get tired, vigorous arm movement will help keep you going at a decent pace. Exercises that build upper body strength are good. You have to train your muscles to be strong.

It is at this most spread-out phase of the stride that loss of contact with the ground may happen. Loss of contact and/or bent-knee walking is sometimes done by individuals who have yet to learn and practice proper technique.

Train your mind to help you walk. It has the power to shut you down or keep you going.

Don't tense or pull in your stomach muscles while walking fast. This restricts oxygen intake and your ability to relax.

A longer stride helps your toes point upward when your heel makes contact. The more your foot lands underneath you, the flatter the angle your toes will be to the ground. A clawing, pulling, and pushing action of the calves, ankles, and toes against the ground will help steadily thrust you forward. This clawing action works well when combined with strong heel pulling.

It has always been easy for me to hyperextend back into my knee joints. This move doesn't come as easily and naturally to all who enter competitions, however, especially older men.

TIPS ON TEACHING

I like to teach beginners by first demonstrating correct technique and then having them try to copy what I've done. I want them to get the feeling of progressing from their casual style of walking to the much quicker style of fast walking.

As I watch everyone give it a try, I see some catching on better than others. I take those having trouble and have them walk a few feet behind and off to my side so they can clearly observe and copy my hip, knee, and arm movement. I feel that one-on-one instruction brings the best results for all who are just starting out.

Having new walkers attempt a few short sprints of 30 to 40 yards will sometimes cause them to do it right. Proper style automatically happens to some when they stop trying to think about the mechanics of what they're doing and just walk as fast as they can. As soon as I see them shift into the fast-walk style, I ask if they could feel the difference. They always say yes. They know their legs are moving more quickly and much more efficiently. Once you experience the unique hip and knee coordination of fast walking, you don't lose it. From there you practice to perfect it and improve the speed and distance you can go.

I've had people who could not jog once or twice around a quarter-mile track fast walk continuously for a full mile the first time they tried it. Of course, they were going slow, but they were getting beneficial exercise for at least 15 to 20 minutes. It's the smooth and quick-step efficiency of fast walking that allows the out-of-shape person to move at the speeds and distances needed to improve their health.

Some beginners find it difficult to learn correct style in a group situation. There are just too many distractions. It's not until they get out and practice by themselves that they learn to perform what they've seen and been told.

Beginners often overdo arm pumping by hunching their shoulders or bringing their arms up too high. Sometimes they swing their hips off to the side too much rather than turning them straight to the front and rear. All fast walkers need to keep their feet landing on or alongside a straight line.

To get more speed out of your legs, use your hips and arms to help whip them forward with each step.

Drive your knees a little downward as you bring them forward so that they, and your feet, are kept close to the ground. Too high of a knee action when trying to move fast can easily cause your lead foot to swing too high as it reaches out for the ground. When this happens, there is a good chance the forward foot won't be able to touch down before the rear foot is pulled off the ground. Competent judges will detect a bouncing or floating action to your feet and may disqualify you for loss of contact.

The forward swinging shoe will come close to nicking the ankle bone of the planted leg.

This photo shows the author in Viareggio, Italy, in August 1967, moving all-out at the end of a 20-km match against Spain and Italy, which he won in 1:28:18, a personal record.

There are those who do just about everything perfectly the first time out. These natural fast walkers are almost always women. Their bodies have a fluency and grace just right for the sport. It's their uninhibited hip roll and easy knee bracing (hyperextension) that does it. Those with good style make excellent demonstrators. I like to have them fast walk for the group so I can point out what they're doing that makes them look so good and move so efficiently. Some men have tighter hips. They need more stretching work and technique walks before mastering a fluid hip roll and correct front-to-rear turning action. Suppleness and efficiency are necessities all fast walkers need to continually work on.

Many quit endurance sports after a while because they get bored with them. Try to give your students enough to think about and work on so that they won't lose interest in the physical fitness activity of fast walking. The more interested they stay in what they're doing, the longer they're likely to continue doing it.

All shapes and ages learn the art of fast walking at a physical fitness class.

Going Downhill

When I want to move downhill fast, I lean my body forward a bit and let gravity do some of the work. This won't feel like the natural thing to do; you'll want to lean back a bit. Roll your hips and take short, quick steps. Whip your legs out in front of you to catch your forward fall as you build up momentum.

Downhill fast walking will give your knees, hips, and lower back a bit of a pounding because of the extra shock to those joints. Keep your steps smooth and controlled so you don't end up in pain or bounce yourself off the ground. If a hill is too steep, you'll need to lean back more.

Be sure to use correct hip movement and knee straightening when fast walking up- or downhill. The English, who invented race walking, have often held some of their most important races on hilly courses to test the uphill and downhill techniques and abilities of their "style" walkers.

CLOTHING AND FOOTWEAR

Clothes for fast walking should be loose enough to provide continuous freedom of movement; if they are too tight or not clean enough, they will cause painful irritations that could ruin a workout or race. A skin lubricant such as Vaseline can be a big help at times.

Don't let the lack of a sweat suit keep you from training. Use old clothes. For the first six months I was in the speed-walking sport, I trained and warmed up for my track meets and road races in an old pair of jeans and a sweater. Thrift stores and garage sales offer a good variety of workout clothes at very low prices. Good-quality shoes with a lot of wear left in them can sometimes be found. However, always buy quality shoes that fit well, even if they are secondhand. New shoes will provide the best cushioning and support.

Many walkers wear whatever running shoes feel good to them. Comfortable, casual leather shoes are sometimes used with good results after they have been broken in. Many shoes from other sports also work well. Even though there are now quite a few quality shoes made just for walking, I've successfully used various running shoes and other sports shoes for training and racing. One of my all-time favorites is the aerobic dance shoe.

Good shoes with lots of soft padding are nice to walk in because they feel so comfortable. The more expensive shoes are lighter weight and let you swing your legs forward a bit easier. Shoes that provide support, fit well, and are lightweight always improve your leg speed and ability to walk farther. Shop for shoes that feel the most comfortable, give you good protection, and are the most functional for your individual fast-walking style, fitness level, and body weight.

If you find shoes you really like for fast walking, stock up on them. The company that makes that model just might discontinue making them after a year or two. Athletic shoe companies are constantly designing and manufacturing new styles of walking shoes. The pictures and descriptions of many in magazines look and sound good. Check them out now and then in shoe stores to see how they feel. Try them on and take some quick steps in them before deciding to spend your money.

Some people like to do their fast and slow walks in street shoes.

Keep your training and racing shoes well repaired. I have over a half dozen pairs of shoes that I've saved and rebuilt over the years just for special racing situations. They have lasted for a long time because I wear them only for important events or when I'm trying to walk my fastest in a time trial. One pair that still works well was given to me at the 1964 Olympics in Tokyo.

One of the most important features of any fast-walking shoe is a strong heel area, or counter. Its support, stability, and protection will also aid your safety and efficiency. If the shoe has a weak heel area, faulty foot strike will soon cause it to crush over onto its side. Too much sideways slope, or crown, to the surface you're walking on will also help crush your shoes over in their heel areas. Once a shoe is crushed over, you may be able to salvage it by carving off enough of the bottom to make it flat again.

You may want to alter the heels and soles of your shoes a bit so that they can help you land

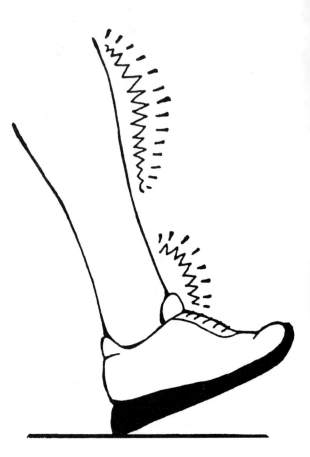

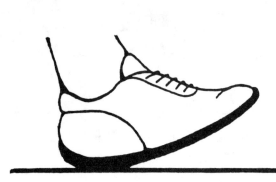

A strong heel counter is best. If you are having shin soreness, try fast walking in shoes with rounded heels. This lets you roll from heel contact down onto the sole of your shoe with less strain to your ankles and shins. Rounded heels should help you avoid excess shin and ankle soreness. Once your shins and ankles have been strengthened, you may find a squared-off heel more to your liking.

Don't be shy about taking a knife or grinding wheel to a pair or two of your athletic shoes. After you've rounded their heels, reinforce and protect them with a few coats of Shoe-Goo. To help improve your speed, efficiency, and comfort, learn to customize your shoes, especially those you plan to race in. Experience will teach you what feels and works best.

The edge of a hard, square heel can force the sole of your foot to collapse to the ground quicker as your body weight drops onto it. When this happens, it puts extra strain and pain on the ankle tendons and shin muscles.

Bending the knee and landing more flat-footed will help eliminate this strain, but when racing you must always use the more efficient and legal technique of straight-leg landing.

Too much padding can throw your high-speed coordination off a bit, absorb some of your pulling power, and cause instability in the heel area when it breaks down.

The extra bulk of an elevated heel can cause high-speed fast walkers to drive their knees a bit higher as they quickly swing their legs forward. Slightly higher knee drive will help float fast walkers up, off, and over the ground during many of their steps. However, with practice, you can get used to various heel heights.

A good pair of shoes is your most important piece of equipment.

and roll along the outside edges of your feet. Since good athletic shoes are usually fairly expensive, I try to get as much wear out of them as possible. The uppers usually hold up well; it's the bottoms that eventually need repair and realignment. Compare the wear patterns on the bottoms of your shoes to see if they are the same. If they aren't, try to figure out what you should do to make them equal.

Low, well-rounded heels help prevent the shin soreness many beginners experience. Training or racing shoes with $\frac{1}{4}$- to $\frac{1}{2}$-inch heels often cause shin soreness. Heels are a lot easier on shins after you've cut them down or after a few weeks of fast walking have worn them down and rounded them off. Higher heels might cause other leg, hip, back, and technique problems. Conversely, some fast walkers might find higher heels a big help.

Heel height also affects your stride length. Experiment with different heights and shoe styles to find out which best suit your technique at various speeds and distances. This can change with time as your fitness and technique improve.

You should have your legs examined to see if they are the same length. If they aren't, a podiatrist can make a heel-lift insert for whichever foot may need it. Trying a heel lift out for a while is the only way to find out if it might alter your stride enough to actually cause more harm than good. It's best to have potential problems taken care of before you begin your fast-walking program. If you don't, you might develop pains and strains in your legs, hips, and lower back. You don't want to take the chance of developing technique and balance problems from poor foot support. A sports podiatrist will be able to test you and make custom-made arch supports with, if need be, a heel-lift insert built into them. I got my first pair back in 1956 and feel they've been helpful over the years.

For racing, I like a snug shoe. Pulling my heels back into the ground helps eliminate most of the pressure tighter shoes have on the fronts and tops of my toes. For important races of 10 kilometers and longer, I wrap three to six layers of adhesive tape over my heels. These adhesive tape heel cups help eliminate friction and add support. Vaseline on the tops and fronts of toes and between them

Distance racing, such as this 50-km track race, demands quality footwear.

takes care of the hot spots that can cause blisters. Toenails need to be well trimmed.

When it comes to racing, you need a good, fast racing shoe. I like shoes with thin bottoms and rounded heels for short, fast races and shoes that are more built up for longer events and training. I think that too much padding absorbs a bit of my heel-pulling and toe-pushing energy. Because of race walking's low impact to the ground, not much padding is needed. Most synthetic tracks are cushioned enough that you can safely wear very light, thin-soled shoes in short races. If your feet are taking a pounding because you are over-weight, shoes with extra padding will help.

For short races out to 10 kilometers, I rarely wear socks. Without socks, my high-speed walking feels a bit quicker and more efficient. Any friction areas can be taken care of with adhesive tape and Vaseline. It's best to wear socks in short races if your shoes are not snug fitting and you're com-peting on a surface where small stones or other debris might get in your shoes. For longer events and most training sessions, I like socks for extra padding and protection. Experiment with some sockless speed sessions to see how they feel and make you move.

One additional accessory you may want to consider is a pair of sunglasses. Wearing sun-glasses on bright days helps keep your face and neck muscles relaxed by eliminating squinting, and they also make you feel as though it's cooler, because you don't see the sun at its strongest.

Training

As with any sport, the basics of fast walking are simple, but when you become dedicated to perfecting your technique, you'll soon come to realize that it can be more complicated and challenging than you thought, with plenty of fine points to improve your performance. Practice is necessary to perfect your style and improve health. A solid base of training helps prevent injury and gives you the endurance needed for maintaining a fast pace.

TRAINING SESSIONS

Following someone else's training program might help you improve and keep you training regularly. Fitness magazines are always coming up with new articles on ways to train, race, eat, and lose weight. Because everyone is not the same, you should experiment with different ways to train. Trial and error will show you what works best for you. You may find it better to determine your own speeds and distances, either before you start your workout or while you are doing it. Some find it best to plan and write down their future training and racing sessions, and then try sticking to that plan the best they can. I like the convenience of being able to step out of my front door, look at my wristwatch, and hit the roads and sidewalks for a specific amount of time. One-hour to 90-minute walks through or near my neighborhood make up the majority of my training efforts. When training for an important contest, I usually spend more time thinking about what I need to accomplish before I hit the road or track.

The lessons you learn through trial and error are more likely to be remembered and put to good use in future races and workouts. Self-improvement helps you develop confidence in your capabilities and provides the incentive to continue. Getting yourself physically and mentally strong enough to fast walk for a half or full marathon of 26.2 miles while using good technique and quickness all the way will give you plenty to be proud of.

Because our bodies were designed to walk, learning how to walk fast should not be difficult. Once beginners have studied the basics of fast walking, it might be best for them to take their new knowledge and practice it by themselves for a few weeks. I've always liked to train alone because I can concentrate more on my form and effort.

In racing, there are always distractions; try not to let them cause you to lose the concentration, technique, and effort that you have practiced in your training. Mental and physical effort will always be needed for your best racing performances. Excellent style lets you move your legs quickly, but superior fitness is required to retain that leg speed for longer and longer distances. Getting fit enough to walk the second half of a race as fast as or even faster than the first half is quite an accomplishment. You don't have to kill yourself during a race, however. Many fitness walkers compete at a pace that is comfortable or only slightly tiring for them. Even the best race walkers sometimes take it easy during parts of their less important competitions.

The amount of slow and fast walking and the specific exercises and stretches you should do for your warmup depend on the intensity and length of effort that is to follow. How much time you have and weather conditions are also factors. Many like to warm up with a mixture of easy running and fast walking at various speeds.

Just as workouts change, so will your warmup routines. When stepping to the starting line, you want your body's balance, flexibility, and muscular and breathing coordination to be as ready as possible. This is especially true if the race is short (1 mile to 5 kilometers) and you plan on going out fast. Standing with your legs slightly bent and vigorously pumping your arms back and forth for 10 to 20 seconds helps get them ready to go. The right warmup for you is something you'll eventually work out for yourself. Intelligent experimentation will show you the best way to get yourself ready. Learn from the mistakes you make.

Let your present health, fitness, and age determine what kind of training schedule to follow. Since fast walking is such a smooth, low-impact activity, you can begin with sessions that are long and vigorous enough to be of value to your health. Don't start out so fast that you quickly get out of breath. Go at a comfortable pace. Always remain aware of your technique. Start slowly and increase your training gradually. Let how you feel be your guide from day to day. It's nice to combine strength and health building with pleasure.

It's best for beginners to start out with 20-minute to half-hour fast walks. From there they can progress up to and beyond an hour by adding a few more minutes of training each week. Mixing strolling with fast walking is a good way to help get used to longer fast-walking sessions. You should still put a fair amount of effort into your strolling. Slow walks are good for physical and mental recovery. After a few of these slower sessions, you should be eager to resume the challenge and exertion of faster walks.

Even during your faster walks, try to stay somewhat relaxed. Relaxation means to slow down and back your effort off just enough to keep the pace tolerable. Your effort level should be strong enough to maintain a high rate of leg speed while still keeping you in control of efficient and legal technique and proper body balance.

Don't be discouraged if you get out of breath quickly. This happens naturally to even the fittest athletes when they start out fast. The amount of oxygen debt an athlete can tolerate usually determines how fast a pace he or she maintains. Those fit enough to handle it better are able to push themselves harder and longer. The fitter you get,

Many competitors want to know their lap times so they can figure out how fast, or not so fast, they are going.

the longer and better you'll be able to deal with both respiratory and muscular stress.

I find my breathing coordination to be at its worst right from the start of a hard, steady effort. Those first 20 to 30 minutes are always the toughest to get through. After that, my respiratory system becomes more harmonious with the rest of my body, and I feel more comfortable all the way to the end of my session, even if I pick up the pace. This renewed breathing coordination is known as getting your second wind. If you are vigorously fast walking a distance of 3 miles or less, there won't be time for you to get your second wind. You'll just have to bear the discomfort of your effort until you slow down or stop.

Whenever you find yourself getting out of breath, you may want to experiment with different breathing patterns. Try to keep your upper stomach (diaphragm) area relaxed by pushing it out as you inhale. If you are in the habit of pulling your stomach in, you will probably tense those muscles while fast walking. Holding in your stomach can help you look better, but tense stomach muscles slow you down because they restrict your oxygen intake. Expand and push your diaphragm area out when inhaling. This helps you take in more air with each breath.

If you plan on moving quickly from start to finish, it's best to do warmup and cooldown routines of easy fast walking and various stretches for at least 10 to 15 minutes. A few 40- to 60-yard accelerations before you start will also help get your muscles and breathing going.

Whatever stretches you do should be done gently. Sudden moves made with stiff and cold muscles can cause injury. It's best to walk slowly for a few minutes before stretching. My favorite fast-walking strength and flexibility exercises are shown and explained in chapter 3. They will help improve your fitness, speed, and technique. For fast walking, the most important muscles to stretch are the large ones on the back of the thighs (hamstrings) and calves. They do most of the work of moving you.

If you plan to make it a slow session, don't spend the time warming up. Just get out there and enjoy yourself. Some walkers warm up by starting out slowly, then push their pace when they feel it's safer. They use slower fast walking to prepare their muscles and breathing for a harder effort.

Getting dressed and out the door is often the toughest part of a training session. Just get out there and do something! You'll feel better physically and emotionally if you do. Don't be lazy. If you need to go slowly, try to stay out a little longer. Work must be done if you are serious about future fitness or having good races. Getting really fit takes a lot of discipline on your part.

On days when you don't feel like getting out there, start out slowly. After a mile or two, you should begin to feel good enough to pick up the pace here and there, or all the way to the finish. Even though getting to the finish can be a real chore, all that extra exertion and perseverance will give you a nice feeling of fulfillment for the rest of your day. If you do happen to finish strong and are moving well, don't hesitate to extend your workout. Nothing says you have to stop once you've accomplished what you started out to do.

Listening to a small radio or cassette player during walks can help get you out and keep you going when your incentive is low and the effort becomes boring. Inspiring music and informative talk can be a big help at getting you through longer workouts. If you use this kind of training aid, fasten it onto your head or body so that it doesn't interfere with your vigorous arm swinging.

If a workout isn't going well, stop, stretch, and rest for a few minutes. You don't have to be racing to enjoy the fitness benefits of fast walking. If things really go poorly, pack it in for the day. You can make up for it the next day if necessary. Some days will be better than others.

Moving steadily toward a fitness goal is the best and quickest way to get there. Too much speed and effort can set you back if you allow it to break you down. If you begin to feel muscular or respiratory strains, you can relax those specific areas a bit or see whether you can tolerate the effort. When training on a long circular or out-and-back course, try to allow yourself enough energy to return to where you started. There have been times when I've fallen apart so badly,

I've had to hitchhike or slowly trudge back to my car or home. I started those sessions with too much boldness and hope, and not enough common sense.

Some find it easier to do a quality workout if they have a training partner or two. But then, finding someone to go with you won't always be easy. In many situations, it will be impossible. It's best to learn how to train on your own, because you are going to be alone with your thoughts and efforts in most of your races. Your main objective in a race is to eventually be alone and out in front when you get to the finish line. You should work to open up as much distance between yourself and as many of the other competitors as possible. There will be plenty of time for socializing after the event is over.

Other than being very fit, good speed and endurance come from paying strict attention to how efficiently you flow over the ground. Even the fittest athletes must continually be aware of their balance and how the various parts of the fast-walk movement can best be used to keep them going at a fast pace. The faster you try to walk, the more you need to think about and actually perform the things that keep your legs moving quickly and somewhat easily. With practice, much of this will become automatic. As your level of fitness improves, so will the speeds and distances you'll be able to handle.

Putting extra effort into your walking will both reward and inspire you if it produces good speed. It's discouraging to push yourself and still produce slow results. When hard effort doesn't move you as fast as you feel it should, look at lack of conditioning, excess weight, and inefficient technique as reasons. As you master the rhythmic flow of fast walking, it should be an exhilarating experience. The personal satisfaction that comes from giving your all to a task will be one of your greatest rewards.

Heart, lung, and muscular endurance take time and work to build. Fast race walks against time and distance every week or two help check progress. Once you get in shape, it's best to stay in shape; then you can go on to improve, a little bit at a time. The time, patience, and work you

devote to your health will be well worth it. Make the time needed to take a walk or do some form of exercise every day.

TECHNIQUE DRILLS

Overemphasizing different parts of fast-walking movement while training, and even racing, is a good way to strengthen and perfect them, and it also makes time pass more quickly. This is usually done for distances of 50 yards to a quarter mile, at a stronger or faster pace.

This walker demonstrates excellent form in sitting back into the hip and knee joints of his supporting leg. Note the low shoulders and forward lean from the ankles.

You could begin by overemphasizing a strong ankle and toe action of pulling and pushing the ground underneath and behind you. Keep it up for a minute or two as you move down the road or around a track. This forceful "clawing" action helps maintain forward ankle lean and smooth glide over the ground.

Next, work your arms more vigorously for a minute or two. Experiment with various arm movements to determine which ones help you walk your fastest while tiring you the least.

Try over-rotating your hips back and forth with each step to take extralong strides. Pumping your arms across your chest also helps turn your hips. Make your stomach, lower back, and hip muscles feel the stretch of those overstrides. This kind of work also improves hip flexibility and helps strengthen muscles in the hip, stomach, and lower back. You'll be getting healthier, stronger, and thinner with every exaggerated step.

Keep in mind that if you wish to compete, you must develop the front-to-rear hip-turning technique in order to exhibit the classic heel-and-toe foot action judges love to see. As discussed in chapter 1, strides with good hip turning land the lead leg out in front of the walker's center of gravity and on its heel with toes pointed well upward. Hip turning also forces the rear leg and toes to stay back and down on the ground an instant longer. All race walkers need to master proper hip turning because it helps to keep them down on the ground during high-speed efforts. However, too much hip turning during very fast race walking can interfere with leg movement efficiency and may cause loss of contact. Rapid back-and-forth hip turning must always be controlled.

Another drill is to make an effort to really dig your heels back into the ground with each step. Be sure your knees are straight at the same instant the heel hits. Keep your steps smooth at all speeds. This drill is a good one to practice while going uphill, because it builds the pulling power of the muscles on the back of your thighs. Pulling power is very important for walking fast and far.

Practice rolling along the outside of your feet and legs to see how this improves your leg speed and efficiency. If you deliberately overdo this by

Overstriding is an excellent strength and flexibility exercise.

taking shorter steps and crossing your feet over the straight line, you should feel a good stretch along the outside of your hips. Repeating this crossover drill for 30 to 50 of every 100 yards will help loosen your hips.

During every fast-walking step, you should experience a sitting back and down into the hip joint of the lead leg as it comes in underneath and behind you. This hip rolling and dropping action also helps swing the opposite leg quickly forward.

For a leg-speed drill, shorten your stride length and arm swing, using only hip roll to increase your rate of steps to the maximum. Don't do any front-to-back hip turning. This should feel like a prancing motion once you get going. Be careful not to drive your knees up too high as you snap them quickly forward, so that you don't break contact with the ground. Stay as smooth as possible. Time and count your steps for 1 minute to see how close you can get to 200 steps per minute.

A similar drill involves leaning forward from your ankles. The forward lean will shorten your strides so that within a few steps your heels will feel as if they are hitting the ground nearly underneath you. Your hips will continue their usual rolling motion for leg speed, but they won't be turning from front to rear as much. Pump your arms more parallel to the sides of your body, rather than across your chest in a pattern that would promote back-and-forth hip turning. Push off your toes and snap your knees forward to aid and maintain the leg speed of these quick, shorter steps.

Work on whipping your hind leg quickly forward with each step while keeping the knee and foot low. Those with a running background often have a tendency to carry their knees a bit too high when swinging them forward. Your feet should just clear the ground as they pass each other. Try to avoid overtwisting your heel and leg to the inside as you push the ground away with your toes.

Also avoid tightening the large muscles above the kneecap just before your heel lands or as it is pulling the ground back. Exaggerated flexing of frontal thigh muscles can force the knee into enough of a bent position to make it illegal. You should find that the faster you walk, the easier your knees will snap back into the classic straight or hyperextended position.

Constantly check that your body balance is aiding your forward momentum. Stay smooth and fluid. Glide along with very little impact to your legs and feet. When fast walking, you should feel as if your feet are barely striking the ground.

Experience the increase in speed and efficiency that these drills on various parts of the fast-walk movement are able to produce. They can be done separately or combined. Some will feel easier to do than others. It usually takes a few of each

to feel more comfortable with the coordination, speed, and effort they require. The difficult ones should eventually be practiced more. Overturning hip action is tough for many people because of the extra hip and lower-back flexibility needed.

Use these exaggerated moves, and any you wish to create, to perfect your technique, leg speed, and stamina. Doing them longer and faster will be goals worth mastering. They can also be used to offset any boredom that may set in during training and racing sessions. Short bursts of style help get you out of any slow ruts you may find yourself slipping into now and then. Keep your face, neck, and hands relaxed at the start of and during your faster technique accelerations. Always keep them smooth and controlled from speedup to slowdown.

The extra concentration and effort needed for doing these technique drills will also come in handy during races. Good racing requires a lot of physical and mental energy. Along with the efforts of pushing yourself and working on effective style, you must also be aware of what these efforts are doing to you so that you can try to continue them or improve them. Fast racing performances will always require more concentration and effort. The challenge is in building the stamina and technique needed to maintain a fast and legal pace over the entire distance you race. To walk fast in your races, you should walk fast in at least a quarter to one-third of your practice miles. Speedy sessions are more beneficial to your heart, lungs, and muscular system.

If you push yourself hard enough, fast walking can be a very demanding sport. Those who train the smartest and hardest develop into the best competitors.

ADDING VARIETY

Putting variety into your exercise program is a great way to eliminate boredom. Vigorous fast walking gives your entire body a complete workout. Being imaginative and spontaneous with most of your walks may be the best way to make sure you start and finish them. Challenge yourself by gradually increasing the speeds and distances you walk. Set new goals to keep yourself interested.

A training spin on a dirt trail. You can experiment with a variety of speeds and technique drills during such sessions, but watch where you step.

Mix up your fast walks by practicing good style at various speeds. Appreciate the joy of physical movement regardless of how uninspiring your course may be. Practice stretching and working different muscle groups as you move along.

Overemphasizing hip turning and strong arm swinging are favorites of mine.

During your walks, work on how you are moving, where you're going, or a combination of both. If you are stuck on a boring course, like a track, parking lot, or treadmill, concentrate on your technique to help make your time and effort pass. If walking on a pretty course or exploring a new one, watching the scenery will help the miles slip by.

If possible, use a variety of scenic and challenging (hilly) courses to train on from time to time. Sometimes I'll drive to a nice park, good track, or country road for a change. I don't care to be bothered by cars and people, but their presence can motivate me to use better form and effort. If you're training on a road, always walk facing into the traffic so that you can see any vehicles coming.

Even though the grass of parks and athletic fields is just fine, I like to do some overstriding and power walking on the perimeters of golf courses if I can keep from being chased off. Power walking, to me, is where I use good style and put more strength and stretch into each step, rather than focusing on speed. Workouts on grass are a nice change of venue once in a while.

Watch that you don't trip on anything when moving over rough surfaces. Because of fast walking's hip rolling and dropping action, your feet skim very close to the ground as they swing forward. It's easy to stub a toe, so look where you're stepping. Smooth, hard surfaces make the best courses.

Workouts in the evening and into the darkness of night can be an invigorating experience for those wanting to add some variety to their training. I've found it easier to concentrate on my fast walking in the dark because I don't have as many distractions. The seclusion of darkness makes it easier for me to get lost in my own world of technique, effort, and all sorts of motivating fantasies. Another benefit of training at night or late or early in the day is avoiding the burning heat of the sun. Job hours or school schedules often necessitate working out during times of little or no sunlight. If you do train in the dark, try to walk over a smooth surface or a surface you are familiar with so that you don't stub a toe or turn an ankle.

Fast walking, like other vigorous exercise, can create sore muscles and joints. This soreness can often be eased or eliminated by improving one's race-walking technique. Strive to move along quickly with a style as efficient as you can make it.

SPEED TRAINING

Speed training about every third workout will reward you with noticeable results after a few weeks. Accelerations of all sorts can be thrown into your slower fast walks anytime you feel the need. I like to do accelerations after 20 to 30 minutes of steady training. By that time, I'm well warmed up and not likely to strain anything.

Once you're well warmed up, fast walk six to ten accelerations for 1 to 2 minutes each. Use a few minutes of slower fast walking in between each to recover. Quicken and shorten your recovery pace so that you force your muscles and lungs to work while they are still in a state of fatigue. This is hard work, but it will help you get fit and used to the rigors of racing.

One of my best workouts is to sprint the straightaways of a track and recover on the turns with a pace that is still fairly quick. Three- to 5-mile sessions twice a week really help build speed and endurance. This workout can also be done on a road course if you don't have a decent track near you.

Sprints of various times or distances can make up part or all of your speed-training sessions. Use a variety of flat and hilly courses. If you're serious about racing, you need to practice fast and legal race walking on uphills and downhills, even though the majority of your races will be held on fairly flat courses.

RECOVERY

Try to keep moving after you've finished a hard workout or race. A combination of easy fast walking, stretching, and strength-building exercises for 10 to 15 minutes will keep your muscles from getting stiff. As part of my cooldown, I sometimes jump right into some sort of physical work that needs doing around my house. A good walk should put you in the mood to do other work.

To help you recover from strenuous workouts, drink water, cover yourself, massage your body, and rub ice on any sore areas. If you have sore, stiff muscles and joints after training, a hot shower within half an hour of finishing will help, as will massaging them. Hot showers and hot drinks are also good at restoring you after you've been out in the cold.

If a walk takes a lot out of you, you need to take it easy for the next day or two. One or two hard days followed by one or two easy days has become a popular and beneficial method of training today. Trial and error will reveal the pattern of hard and easy days that works best for you. This pattern of hard and easy walks will change as you get fitter. Sometimes it's good to practice a totally different activity to help the mind and body recover, such as swimming, roller skating, riding a bike, or playing the piano.

TAKING NOTES

I've kept a personal training diary since 1965 but wish I'd started when I first began the sport ten years earlier. If you keep a diary, it needs to be an honest record of what you did, the effort used, and how you felt. It's good to have the details of past racing experiences and tactics in case you need to review them. Any pains or injuries should also be noted so you can recall if they were diagnosed and treated correctly. Weather conditions, special exercises, and problems with your shoes are important. Other useful information can include what you have eaten, how you were affected by what you ate, and how much you weighed. Any experiments with or changes in your technique should also be recorded. Write more details on race days.

Use your diary to help motivate your daily workouts. Jot down thoughts on what you hope to accomplish and how you are progressing. Add some personal experiences as they happen. It will make good reading years from now.

Some of your clearest thinking and most creative ideas will come during your training sessions. If you carry pen and paper in a pocket, quick notes will make sure you preserve your best thoughts. You can easily jot them down while you're quickly and efficiently moving your legs.

Exercise and Diet

STRETCHES AND EXERCISES

A routine of stretches and strength-building moves before and after your walks is a good habit to get into. Simple exercises like situps, pushups, pullups, knee bends, and calf raises are excellent and don't require special equipment. Be inventive as you make up exercises that specifically work the different parts of the body needed for fast walking. Stomach and lower-back exercises are great for those wishing to improve their health and ability to walk fast and far. Lots of stomach work will help slim your waist down.

Lower-back and hip flexibility work is important to proper race-walking technique and legality. Competitors who lack flexibility are often disqualified because of using a bent-knee hiking style. With flexibility exercise and practice, bent-knee walkers should be able to correct their technique.

I find it necessary to practice a variety of exercises before going to the starting line of a fast race. Fast efforts need a warmup of walking at various speeds and some good stretching work. These moves are also excellent after a hard training session or race to help eliminate soreness and aid recovery.

Most of the stretches and strength exercises presented here were developed from personal experience. Some were learned from other athletes and coaches, from this country and others. All of these moves will help you develop the specific fast-walking strength and flexibility needed for better training, racing, and recuperation.

It's up to you to decide when, where, and how many of these different exercises and stretches to do. They will benefit you anytime you do them. Try them all to see how they affect how you feel and how you walk. You can also invent and

Fast walking exercises the entire body.

experiment with whatever stretches and power builders you think may help you feel and function better.

The illustrations on this page show my favorite series of warmup and recovery stretches.

First, lean against a wall to stretch your calves. By bending your knees a little, you also stretch the Achilles tendons more. Keep your heels flat on the ground.

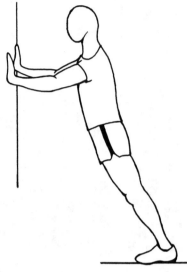

Second, place your leg out in front of you, and brace your foot at the bottom of the wall. While in this spread-out position, rotate your hips back and forth a few times as far as you can stretch them. Keep both legs straight.

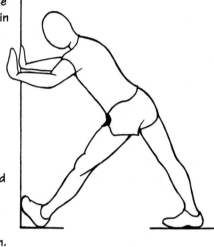

Third, with most of your weight on your rear leg, and the hip of your front leg turned well forward, slowly drag your heel all the way back to your rear foot. You should feel a nice stretch all the way up the entire length of your leg as you slowly pull your heel back. Turn your hip to the rear as you complete the move.

Try to keep the heel of the rear foot down with toes pointed directly forward. Repeat these hip turns and heel pulls about five times before switching legs.

Knee lifts really work the tendons at the top of your thighs. Pulling your knees up to your chest with your hands for a few steps stretches the butt and groin muscles. This is a good exercise to do while wearing ankle weights. Exaggerated arm swings can also be worked into these moves.

Pushups are great for arm, shoulder, and chest strength. I like to stretch up as far as I can with each effort. After you've straightened your arms, you can lean back on your toes to give your calves a nice stretch. If these moves are tough to do, start out doing them from your knees.

Repeated lifts of one leg and then the other really work the butt and lower-back muscles. These lifts also aid hip and back flexibility and strength.

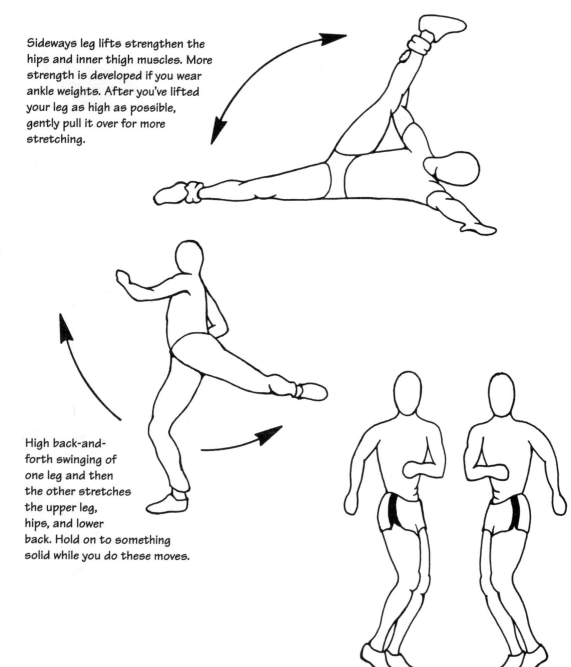

Sideways leg lifts strengthen the hips and inner thigh muscles. More strength is developed if you wear ankle weights. After you've lifted your leg as high as possible, gently pull it over for more stretching.

High back-and-forth swinging of one leg and then the other stretches the upper leg, hips, and lower back. Hold on to something solid while you do these moves.

Rapid back-and-forth twisting works on your hip, lower-back, and stomach flexibility. These moves will also help to loosen your lower breathing area, or diaphragm. They are good to do just before the start of a fast race.

Various arm moves with dumbbells build arm, shoulder, chest, and back strength and stamina. You can do all sorts of valuable work with these training aids.

The chinup is a superior strength builder for arms and shoulders. This move really helps develop the power and endurance needed for long periods of arm pumping.

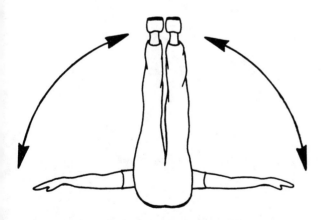

Keep your legs together and fairly straight as you lower them to one side, and then up and over to the other side. Slow and controlled back-and-forth movements help build power and suppleness into your hip turning and lower back.

This stretch feels good on your lower back. It also stretches your shins and thighs. Try not to fall asleep while in this relaxed position.

Arching up strengthens and stretches the lower back and stretches the shins. Use your back and arms to help muscle yourself up and down.

Here's another fine lower-back and hamstring stretch for you to try. If you have a free hand or two while holding various stretches for 15 to 30 seconds, try massaging some of your relaxed muscles.

Twisting your midsection back and forth while hanging from a bar or tree limb is good exercise for hip, stomach, and lower-back flexibility.
    Stationary hanging gives the arms, shoulders, and entire back a beneficial stretch.

This full squat stretches the lower back, quadriceps, and calves. It really feels good within 2 or 3 minutes of finishing a long fast walk.

Here's a fine stretch for the shins and thighs. Watch out for possible knee strain.

Use a steady pull for 15 to 30 seconds to give the shin and thigh muscles a nice stretch.

Back-and-forth leg swings stretch the hips and the muscles on the front and back of the thighs.

The muscles of the inner thigh get a nice stretch from holding this position for at least 30 seconds at a time.

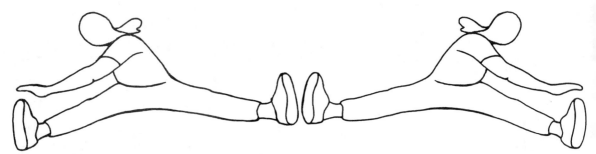

Back-and-forth twisting from the waist loosens lower-back, stomach, and hamstring muscles. If you breathe heavily during these moves, your diaphragm area will get a good workout similar to what it goes through during rapid fast walking. I like to do about a minute of these twists before going to the starting line of a fast race.

Situps strengthen the stomach and lower back. You can also combine them with hip flexor work and hamstring stretches.

Rounding your back and bending your knees helps you do the situp and avoid lower-back strain. Hip muscles get massaged against the floor as you come up and down at different angles.

Raising your legs up and onto your shoulders works your midsection. With each over-and-back move, the back and shoulder muscles get a nice massage against the floor.

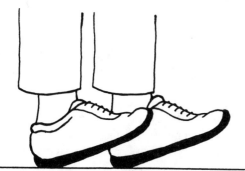

Walking on your heels for 30 seconds to a minute at a time strengthens the shin muscles. This exercise can be practiced anytime and anywhere.

When fast walking in place, pump your arms in a good fast-walk pattern.

FAST WALKING IN PLACE

Fast walking in place is an excellent way to experience the feeling of correct hip, knee, and arm movement. It can be used to warm up, cool down, give the hips a good twisting, and stretch the specific muscles and tendons of fast walking. Pumping 5- to 20-pound dumbbells at the same time will help build upper-body strength and stamina.

Stand with feet together. Sit back into the hip and knee of one leg, then shift your body weight onto your other leg and do the same. This simultaneous hip drop and snapping back into the knee joint from one leg to the other needs to be learned first. After this motion has been mastered, add front-to-rear hip turning. If you keep both feet flat on the ground, you can put more stretch into your hip turning. Hip dropping and twisting is a great exercise before and after workouts, and throughout the day. It's one you can do while watching TV. Be careful not to let your hips sway out from your sides as you move from one leg to the other.

Using ankle weights and small dumbbells as training aids is safe because of race walking's unique hip and knee action and its low impact with the ground.

Watching your style from different angles while walking in place in front of a full-length mirror will give you an idea of what you actually look like. This will help you correct any flaws in your technique.

I like to start beginners out by having them fast-walk in place. All fast walkers will benefit from practicing this drill. If done while slowly bending over and grasping your ankles or shins, it gives your hamstrings, hips, and lower back a good stretching.

USING WEIGHTS

Fast walking doesn't require a lot of weightlifting. If you wish to see what pumping iron can do, go ahead and give it a try for six months to a year. Many people enjoy and benefit from doing a variety of different moves using various weights and exercise machines. Health clubs offer a wide choice of these machines and other equipment. I have a pair of antique brass 15-pound dumbbells I've used for years in an extra effort to strengthen and increase the stamina of my upper body. They are great to muscle around after a walk, or any time of day.

Wearing ankle weights and using light (2- to 5-pound) hand weights is a grand way to combine resistance work and quick walking. Because of fast walking's low impact to feet and legs, have no fear about lugging them around for an hour or two. Ankle weights help you develop the strength you need to pull your trailing leg off the ground and snap it forward. The muscles and tendons at the top and front of your hips get stronger and gain endurance as you walk with heavy shoes and/or ankle weights. Carrying hand weights builds arm and shoulder power and endurance. About once a week I get in the mood to pile on some weights and take a powerful fast walk for an hour or so.

TIRE DRAGGING

Dragging an old tire while fast walking builds strength for hamstring pulling and hip turning; increases the pushing power of your calves, ankles, and toes; improves your fast-walking power and stamina; and gives your lower back a good strength and flexibility workout. It's also one of the best and quickest ways to develop correct knee action.

Even though you will move along at a slow pace, be sure that you use proper technique and are well warmed up. This is not a speed session. The resistance of the tire will eventually, if not immediately, get your knees into the correct straight position with each step.

Use a tire that's not too heavy for you, and stay on level ground. My favorite place to drag a tire is around the outside lane of a track or over adjacent grass. Clean asphalt and concrete grip the tire well, but grass provides the best resistance. If the tire slides too easily or bounces, slow yourself down by walking on grass or adding weight to it. Make yourself work to keep that tire moving. Two sessions per week of 20 to 30 minutes each is a good way to start. An hour should be plenty once you've worked your way up to it. Be careful not to strain yourself; this drill puts a lot of pressure on the hips, legs, and feet. Keep it smooth, and let the resistance of the tire straighten your knees back where they belong.

If you want to improve your hip turning, put the effort into twisting your hip around a little more with each step. The resistance of the tire will do the rest.

DIET

Don't give in to the habit of rewarding yourself by overeating when you've had a few days of good training. Diet experts say that what and how much we eat is 70 to 80 percent more important than the exercising we do. You need to put into your body that which makes you healthy. And always remember to drink plenty of water and juices throughout the day, even if you don't feel thirsty.

On days when circumstances don't allow you to eat or exercise well, don't let it upset you. Call it a rest day and use it to motivate future efforts. If the calories in your body are low due to diet or missed meals, you may have trouble training for more than a semihard half hour. In order to make it through a full hour, you'll have to bear down with a steady, concentrated effort.

What and how much to eat before a strong, fast effort of 1 mile to 10 kilometers is a concern for most beginners. With all the hip rolling and twisting of the stomach and diaphragm, I've found it best to start off with little or no food in my system. Thus the extra energy my body would have had to spend on digesting and assimilating a sizable meal can be used for a faster and stronger performance. Plus, I won't have to suffer the added discomfort of excess food in my stomach. I take sips of water right up to race time to satisfy my hunger pangs. Other people can eat a normal to heavy meal an hour or two before a hard workout or race and still feet fine. And if your walk will be a slow one, it's not as much of a problem.

I've found that if I eat a large meal the night before a hard, early-morning 5- to 10-kilometer race, I'll feel somewhat sluggish for the event. It's best for me to eat a light evening meal. Experiment before race day to determine how much and what kinds of foods work best for you.

For tire-dragging, use a strong, wide belt, a couple yards of rope, and an old tire with a small hole cut through its middle. Wrap a towel under the belt to keep it from chafing you.

IMPROVING RUNNING WITH FAST WALKING

I suggest that serious runners incorporate fast walking into their training programs. Fast walking is a different way of working, stretching, and even resting all the muscles and tendons that runners so often overuse and sometimes injure.

When runners do hard interval workouts, I also feel that it would be safer for them to walk or fast walk between bursts of speed. This gives a stretching and low-impact recovery to the severely used running muscles and tendons.

When fast walking is done well, walkers will smoothly glide along, barely feeling their steps touch the ground. This is why fast walking can safely be done on any hard surface.

Correct hip roll is what gives fast walking its great leg speed and efficiency. Hip action helps act as a shock absorber to the feet, legs, and lower back. When you combine hip rolling with back-and-forth hip turning, you develop the kind of stomach, lower-back, and hip flexibility and stamina that also help your running.

Since many dedicated runners often find it necessary to really push themselves during their training, fast walking allows them to safely satisfy this strong emotional and physical desire. Even though you may feel that Olympic-style walking looks strange, once you've mastered correct technique and done the work it takes to get used to this new way of exercising, you'll be pleased at how fast you can move your legs and how long you can keep them going. You'll discover that fast walking is a great way to get fit and stay fit while allowing your running muscles and tendons to recover from much of their strenuous training and racing efforts.

As with running, the more vigorously you fast walk, the harder your heart, lungs, and muscles have to work. Fast walking helps keep runners from losing the respiratory and cardiovascular fitness they work so hard to develop and maintain. The low impact of fast walking allows you to move quickly and vigorously for fairly long periods of time. The different angles at which the muscles are exercised will feel strange at first but will become more comfortable with a few weeks of practice.

You don't need special athletic equipment and facilities or training partners to enjoy this beneficial cross-training sport. Fast walking can be done before, during, or after a running workout or for your entire training session.

For longer efforts beyond two or three hours, I still avoid eating too much. During strong efforts of two hours or longer, a continuous intake of various sugar products will help keep you going. Liquids should be taken at least by the half-hour mark if you can get them. They are very important on warm, sunny days. The energy your body uses for endurance efforts of two hours or longer comes mostly from the carbohydrates you eat one, two, and three days before. Physical fitness magazines will keep you up-to-date on the latest nutrition theories. After reading and thinking about these ideas, you may wish to try some to see if they work for you.

Racing and Judging

It's natural to eventually want to test yourself after having done the work it takes to learn and consistently practice for an endurance event. You can test your skill and fitness by seeing how quickly you can fast walk over an accurately timed and measured distance. You can do this alone by timing a hard effort on a good track or some other well-measured course. Such time trials are good for those who need some self-confidence before entering a competition. Hard time trials will also give you a good idea of your racing fitness.

If you have a strong desire to compete and can't find a walking race near you, try race walking in a running race. Most runs are well organized and attract a lot of competitors. They will help you have a fast workout and give you the chance to demonstrate this unique fitness activity to others.

If you are going to enter a race, you should be trained enough to use correct race-walking technique every step of the way. Even if fatigue causes you to slow down, you should always maintain proper form.

The 1996 Olympic Games 20-km walk. It's an honor and challenge for judges to be invited to officiate at big international contests like this.

A group of young boys and girls begin a 3-km race as friends and relatives look on. This safe endurance activity is ideal for elementary school gym classes.

RULES

Knowing the rules of race walking will help you understand and perform the event better. Top officials from all over the world get together now and then to discuss and work on these rules. These individuals are all very experienced and dedicated to the cause of protecting our sport and improving its image and credibility. When the international committee refines the rules of race walking, they are convinced that their changes will significantly help the situation and can be enforced without adding complexity to the existing judging procedure.

The national governing body for race walking in America is U.S.A. Track and Field. USATF holds a national convention late each year, always in a different city. Try to attend this annual event when it comes to your part of the country.

Additional booklets on race-walk judging are also available from U.S.A. Track and Field, Box 120, Indianapolis, IN 46206-0120, and the International Amateur Athletics Federation, 17 rue Princesse Florestine, Postal BP359, MC-98007, Monaco.

There are currently only two race-walking rules, and competitive walkers of all abilities need to know and are required to obey them:

1. **Race walking is a progression of steps so taken that the walker makes contact with the ground, so that no visible (to the human eye) loss of contact occurs.**

In other words, the advancing foot has to look like it has touched the ground before the toes of the rear foot have left the ground. Even though a loss of contact that is visible to the human eye is always illegal, experienced race-walk officials do recognize the limitations of judging it. Race

Legal form has to be maintained throughout all competitions. No bent-knee-creeping and leaping here and there as fatigue and loss of concentration begin to challenge you.

If contestants in official races were allowed to walk with bent knees, there would be those who would take advantage of the situation by using their quadriceps to help thrust themselves forward with a shuffling, jogging, creeping style.

walkers must always try to look as if they are not breaking contact with the ground.

2. **The advancing leg must be straightened (not bent at the knee) from the moment of first contact with the ground until in the vertical upright (directly underneath you) position.**

It used to be that your leg was allowed to land slightly bent but had to straighten out by the time it got directly under you. Now the leg must be straight the instant the heel touches the ground. Many officials feel that stricter knee straightening is a big help in improving heel and toe contact with the ground.

Try to have someone observe your walking if you have doubts about how legal your knee action looks. Bent-knee race walking is fairly easy to see. If you can't find anyone who is qualified to help evaluate the legality and efficiency of your form, you might need to attend a clinic or big race, where you'll be sure to learn correct technique. The illustrations in this book should also help.

If possible, try to demonstrate your technique to a judge or two before a race so they can tell you if you have any obvious problems. It's also good to ask judges what they thought of your style after the event is over. Don't be shy about this. Some of the best coaching I've ever received came from judges. Many judges were also good competitors, and some still compete. Judges may be available to answer questions from walkers both before and after a race.

When beginners fail to receive adequate race-walk coaching, they occasionally learn bad habits. Those who try to figure out the mechanics of the Olympic style of walking by themselves have often developed faulty technique. Even though race walking is not difficult to learn, it's best for beginners to get instructions from good literature, a video, or someone with a fair amount of experience. I learned the basics by watching and imitating some good walkers while they warmed up for a 2-mile track race. After the event, a couple of them were kind enough to offer me more specific help. By knowing what the illegal forms of race

For better heel and toe contact with the ground, back-and-forth hip turning should be added to the race walker's continual hip rolling and dropping movement. As the hip of the lead leg turns forward, the hip of the supporting leg will turn to the rear. This action causes the rear foot of the high-speed walker to stay back, and down on the ground an instant longer. As this happens, the heel of the lead foot has more time to make contact.

Forward arm swing that crosses the chest helps create good hip turning. It also helps dissipate much of the upward lifting force that straight back-and-forth arm pumping may create. Combining cross-chest arm pumping with hip turning does take more effort, but will produce a stride that looks more like it has heel and toe contact with the ground.

I feel that all serious competitors should complement their styles with improved hip turning if they wish to hold better contact with the ground and improve the image and credibility of race walking. However, if overdone at high speed it can interfere with the efficiency of your leg movement and even cause you to lose contact. Always keep your hip turning and arm pumping under control.

A wide and contrasting stripe on the side of walkers' racing shorts will help to show the judges how much more contact-improving hip action they are trying to add to their technique. Drawing attention to hip turning might help persuade judges that the doubtful contact of a high-speed walker is good enough not to be given a warning (disqualification). Conscientious competitors realize that they have to develop a high-speed style that should always look fair to the judges.

When the advancing leg lands out in front of the race walker's center of gravity, the foot naturally lands on its heel with toes pointed upward.

Race walkers need to get their heels down before the toes of their rear feet leave the ground. Overstriding at high speed is uneconomical and dangerous because it is tiring and could result in a visible loss of contact.

When the leg speed and efficiency of hip rolling and dropping are combined with the stride lengthening of hip turning, you have the basics for fast, classic/legal-looking race walking. Other requirements are early leg straightening, vigorous arm pumping, flexibility, good balance, and lots of effort. Effort is the key to going fast, far, and fair.

This photo captures the lead foot of the lead walker the instant before his heel touches the ground, at which point his knee will straighten out. Note the knee-straightening action of the walkers behind him. Judges ensure the fairness of races by trying to watch each competitor long enough to determine if he or she is walking legally.

walking look and feel like, you should, with practice, be able to avoid them.

JUDGING

The specially trained race-walking judges try to make sure all competitors are walking legally and therefore competing under equal conditions. The success or failure of a racing program depends on the quality of the judging. They are to make their decisions by themselves and be strict and firm when it comes to making those decisions. Poor or timid judging is very bad for the sport because it can discourage the legal walkers and ruin the event.

A competitor's knee action and ground contact are only to be judged by human eye (glasses are okay).

No camera or video equipment may be used for judging. This is presently considered to be the only practical and fair way to judge. Even though they try their best, the top judges in the world find it nearly impossible to actually see the small losses of contact exhibited by a fast-moving, technically sound, well-conditioned race walker.

29 August 1967, Dusseldorf, Germany: The author winning the United States vs. West Germany 10-km bahngehen (track walk) with a new American record of 44 minutes, 38 seconds.

Official records could only be set on regulation 440-yard or 400-meter tracks back then. Now there is another category that also allows them to be set on accurately measured and officiated road courses.

Be careful not to pump one arm across your body more than the other. Uneven arm movement can twist your upper body a bit to one side as you move along. A slight twist at the waist may disturb your balance and hinder your efficiency. It may also cause lower back pain.

This photo shows good thrusting back into hip and knee joints.

This lead foot is not about to land; it is low to the ground and still swinging forward. As the knee comes forward and straightens out, the toes flex upward an instant before the heel strikes the ground. As the heel lands, the ankle, hamstrings, hips, and arms keep working to move the body quickly forward. It is at this maximum, spread-out, heel-and-toe position that the high-speed race walker either maintains or breaks contact with the ground. Judges like to see the lead leg land on its heel, and out in front of the walker's center of gravity.

Hard heel pulling plus high leg speed may cause the race walker to bounce up off the ground a bit. Walkers fit enough to sustain this combination of speed and power can produce fast results by illegally gaining a few extra inches through the air with each step. However, if the loss of contact is detected by judges, a walker could be disqualified. Competitors must always be in control of their style, especially when they are forcing their pace.

Judging demands a concentrated look for knee straightening and foot contact.

Loss of contact is difficult to judge because it happens so quickly and within such small spaces. Leg straightening is a lot easier to see because of the large area of the knee joint, and the extra time judges have to watch its action. What judges can't see, they can't call. If a walker's technique looks good, judges should have a clear conscience about its being legal. Only official race-walk judges are to decide whether the walker is walking in a manner that does not exhibit a visible loss of contact.

The best place for judges to accurately observe contact and knee action is from the side of the walkers as they pass by. Those 5 to 10 yards on either side of the perpendicular position provide the best and fairest view of what the competitors' feet and knees are doing. For track races, judges

The front and back of a judge's caution sign shows the symbols for loss of contact (left) and bent knees.

RACES FOR AGE GROUPS

Most walking and running races offer five- to ten-year age divisions for their more mature participants. These usually start at age thirty-five for women and forty for men. This Masters or Veterans division has grown in popularity over the years since first beginning in this country in the mid-1960s. A World Championship Track and Field meet is held every other year and is hosted by different countries. Everyone competes in five-year age groups. The men have a 5-kilometer track race and a 20-kilometer road race. Women go at it for 5 kilometers and 10 kilometers on track and road. The entire track meet is open to everyone, regardless of his or her ability. So far there are no qualifying standards. All you have to do is send in your entry form and fee on time, and pay your way to get and stay there. Longer road championships for women (20 kilometers) and men (30 kilometers) are also contested during the years between the championship track and field meets. Giving people a chance to compete within their own five- to ten-year age groups has encouraged many to enter various athletic events for the first time.

A group of 60-year-old women walkers get plenty of exercise and experience in a 5-km race.

Judges need to watch tight turns closely for sudden breaks in form (bent knees and/or loss of contact).

need to position themselves in the outside lanes so that the inside curb does not obstruct the view of the race walkers' feet.

To be disqualified from a race, a competitor must get a disqualification call from a minimum of three different judges for loss of contact or bent knees. These disqualification calls are called warnings. Each judge is allowed to put in *only one* warning (disqualification) call on each walker, no matter how many times he or she sees that walker breaking the contact rule or straight-leg rule. As in baseball, three strikes (warnings) and you're out, except that each strike must come from a different judge.

The judges give a caution to a walker if they feel he or she is in danger of violating the bent-knee rule or the contact rule. Even though these caution calls are given only once, they can be communicated separately if the judge feels the walker deserves both. In other words, a judge can caution a walker twice—once for being in danger of losing contact with the ground and once for being in danger of landing on a bent leg. A walker cannot be disqualified for receiving cautions.

The judges communicate with a walker by using a 6- to 8-inch-wide sign in the shape of a table tennis paddle. On either side of this white paddle, the international symbols for bent knees and loss of contact are drawn with thick black lines. If there is a lack of paddles, the caution calls must be given out verbally. All caution calls are recorded by each judge and passed on to the head judge during or after the competition.

A warning, or disqualification, call is not communicated directly to the walker, but is recorded on a separate card and promptly given to the recorder or head judge. If walkers knew which judge had handed in a warning, they might try to take advantage of the situation the next time that judge came into view. Thus it's best that competitors aren't told when judges hand in warning cards on them during their races. They can find out after the race is over if they wish.

If a competitor is clearly in violation of the contact rule or straight-leg rule, the judge should promptly write up a warning card on that athlete; therefore, no caution for being in danger of losing

An illustration of loss of contact. The rear leg has been snapped forward before the lead foot has made contact with the ground.

Here the author breaks contact with the ground during a 20-km race in Pomona, California.

Hard effort and a 7:15-minute-per-mile pace pull the rear (supporting) leg away before the lead foot can make contact.

Loss of contact can happen when you go fast and try to stay more mentally and physically relaxed than you should. Once again, concentrate and stay in control of what you are doing, especially when racing.

Loss of contact only takes place when the legs are in their most spread-out position. Perfectly legal race walking requires keeping at least one foot on the ground at all times and having both feet on the ground the instant the heel touches or during the maximum spread-out position. Slight loss of contact is impossible to detect; the human eye can't focus on the small spaces under shoes of race walkers as they zip along at three to four steps per second.

Although a 7:15-per-mile pace isn't impressive by today's standards, back in 1969 one judge had the power to disqualify you, so walkers were more cautious about technique and speed.

To help maintain better contact in this race, I shortened my stride by pushing my hips forward and leaning back a bit. Inward twisting of the supporting foot's heel kept my toes on the ground an instant longer and helped keep my back kick low. Lowering the arms and using more back-and-forth hip turning also helped keep my feet down. These techniques are still useful for those with a contact problem.

The fact that camera and video equipment are not used for judging favors the athlete; judges use their eyes and are asked to give the walker the benefit of the doubt.

contact or bending the knee too much is necessary. Judges are not required to first give out a caution before writing up a warning.

In most races, all walkers competing on a lap course are informed about how many warnings they have received by way of a warning posting board set up next to the course. Since intense racing efforts and crowded conditions could make the reading of this board difficult for the walkers as they zip by, the board needs to be large enough for them to see. Whether or not there is a warning board, all warning calls must always be passed on to the head judge as soon as possible so that he or she can deal with any illegal walkers. Smaller races shouldn't worry about providing a warning board if it isn't practical.

If three warning calls come in on the same walker from three different judges, the head judge is the only official allowed to communicate the disqualification to the walker. Although all judges carry a white caution paddle, the head judge is the only judge who also carries and uses a red disqualifying paddle or red flag.

If it's difficult to inform competitors of their disqualification during a race, it must be communicated to them as soon as possible after they finish. Competitors need to realize that if they are not informed about any illegality of their style during the race, they will learn about it soon after they have finished. Thus they must constantly work at keeping their contact and knee action legal.

Race-walking judges make races fair for everyone by disqualifying those who are not competing within the rules. They have the sole authority to determine the fairness or unfairness of the walking. Their combined decisions are final and without appeal.

Judges must never let the past performances of competitors influence their present and future decisions. They are to judge each walker individually. A competitor with marginal legality is not to be compared to someone with superb style. When in doubt, judges are to give the benefit of doubt to the race walker.

It is best if novice judges attend various races to work alongside experienced judges. With enough training, these beginners will be able to judge by themselves and eventually teach others.

The race-walk judges are to get together and select the head, or chief, judge no later than 30 minutes before the start of a race. He or she assigns the other judges to their judging positions around the track or on the road course. The maximum number of judges is six for track races and nine for road events.

If only two judges show up for a race, I suggest the most qualified one should be given the power to give out two warning calls on each walker. If only one judge is present, he or she should have the authority to hand out all three warning calls. These calls would be given at three separate times throughout the race. If no judges show up, the walkers are to be on their best behavior, which is how they are always supposed to compete anyway.

DEVELOPING LEGAL TECHNIQUE

The following sections illustrate and explain correct race-walking technique and what can be done to help make it legal. Judges are only interested in what your knees and feet are doing. By avoiding knee and contact faults, you will save yourself the disappointment and embarrassment of future disqualifications.

Avoiding Loss of Contact

Loss of contact is the toughest infraction to judge because it is difficult for the human eye to actually detect. It happens so quickly and within such small spaces. The eye cannot focus on simultaneous heel and toe contact while the feet are moving so rapidly. However, when the feet start to look like they are floating or bouncing off the ground, the judges take action.

Breaking contact with the ground, or lifting, does happen during hard and high-speed efforts. Even though race walkers should always be concerned about losing contact at any speed, they really don't have to worry about it until they are fast enough to break the 8-minute-per-mile barrier. Walkers are also likely to lose contact when accelerating and when racing around tight turns.

A combination of leg speed, overstriding, and frantic arm pumping floats the author up off the ground as he sprints to the finish line of a 10-mile road race in Pasadena in January 1966. Even the inward twisting of the rear heel didn't prevent loss of contact during this short, all-out sprint. Breaking contact happens naturally at high speeds. Those illegal inches add up when legs move at around 4 steps per second. Very fit race walkers will look smooth and in control while gaining illegal distance. Consequently, their times will be very fast. The fitter they are, the longer they can lose contact and still look good doing it. It's also easy to lose contact with the ground when you combine overstriding with leg speed and fatigue.

Race-walk judges have one of the most demanding jobs in all athletics. They need a lot of experience before they are asked to officiate an international event.

Race walkers should always wear numbers on their backs, rather than just on their fronts. This allows judges to completely focus in on the foot and knee action of the oncoming walkers without having to look for and remember their numbers at the same time. If the number is used only on the front, walkers are often past before a judge can spot the number.

There should be a smooth flow of the body along the ground. The hips, legs, and feet need to smoothly pull and push you forward. You must try to look as if you have one foot on the ground at all times. The advancing leg's heel should land in front of the walker's center of gravity and contact the ground before the toes of the rear foot lose contact. It is at this maximum spread-out heel and toe position that the fast race walker either stays on or comes off the ground. Judges may observe a competitor's bad balance, high arm and shoulder action, lack of hip turning, and high knee action to help them make their decisions. However, only the position of the feet in relation to ground contact, and the angle of the knee of the lead leg, will determine the legality of the walker's movement.

Competitors with very good style usually lose contact when they race walk at high speed. They simply look smoother and in better control, so they get away with it more often.

High forward knee drive takes more energy and can easily thrust the body up and off the ground with both feet at the same time. If combined with very little hip turning and high, strong arm pumping, this prancing kind of style is sure to cause loss of contact. Keep your knees low so

that your feet just clear the ground as they swing forward. Stay in control.

As your hips turn back and forth to help lengthen your stride and keep your feet close to the ground, the heel of your rear foot naturally turns in a bit to the inside as the foot comes up onto its toes. This hip-turning action will help keep your rear foot and back kick low, but it should not be overdone. If it is, you will waste energy, lose efficiency, and possibly develop pain in your knees, hips, and hamstring muscles. You'll also wear out the soles of your shoes more quickly as you grind them against the ground with each step.

Good hip and lower-back flexibility will help you increase your stride length and maintain legality. It also helps you get the heel of your lead leg down before the rear foot is pulled away. Since race walkers lose some of their flexibility with age, you need to continually work on it with various stretching exercises and massage.

It's one thing to do the work required for good hip, stomach, and lower-back flexibility, and another to actually use that flexibility for better heel and toe contact with the ground in a race. Some ignore the extra work that flexibility and hip turning takes in order to gain more leg speed

A prancing style characterized by high forward knee drive (third figure from left) and high back kick (third figure from right) wastes energy and causes loss of contact. Notice the lack of hip turning; the stripe on the side of the shorts is barely moving back and forth. This causes the advancing leg to land too much underneath the walker and the foot to flatten too soon. The loss of contact illustrated here would lengthen the stride by 4 to 7 inches per step. At a leg speed of 200 steps per minute, a lot of illegal distance through the air would soon be gained.

This drawing shows arms and shoulders coming up too high. This will lift the body up and off the ground if done too vigorously. The instant the arms reach their maximum spread-out position is when the legs are also at their maximum spread-out position. If the arms come up too high or the shoulders shrug upward, they will cause the feet to break contact with the ground during their critical heel and toe, spread-out position. Race walkers lose contact when they pull the supporting rear leg off the ground before the advancing foot has the extra instant it needs to make contact. Those who are fit enough can glide along looking quite good to the human eye. At the same time, they are illegally gaining at least 2 to 6 inches through the air per step. As they tire, their form becomes more bouncy and floaty looking. If fatigue or good sense doesn't slow them down, the judges should. Good judging will pull the obvious lifters out.

Judges are to observe the foot contact and leg straightening of each individual walker without comparing it to how anyone else looks. Judges get the best view of competitors by watching them from the side and the worst view from the rear.

Trying to stretch out your stride at high speed is fatiguing and likely to make you break contact with the ground. A normal stride, or one that even looks a bit short, will help you stay on the ground and get past the judges. Don't overdo it; stay in control!

and better racing results. Small losses of contact with the ground are difficult to detect with the human eye. To be on the safe side, practice hip turning to help maintain better contact during high-speed race walking.

At high speeds, the rear leg is usually snapped forward before it gets back to where the calf, ankle, and toes can be of much help in pushing you forward. Sitting back into your hip an instant longer after you have pulled your supporting leg underneath you is a big help in staying on the ground. This turning and sitting-back action helps thrust you forward and gives your calf, ankle, and toes a bit more time to help push you forward.

Even if you're using plenty of hip turning, you can still lose contact during high-speed race walking if you overstride or pull the rear leg off the ground and forward too soon. The fitter and faster you become, the more you need to be aware of how easy it is to break contact with the ground. Hip turning does take more effort, but it

will help you maintain better contact. Speed and technique must always be controlled.

Pressing your hips forward a little helps keep you down on the ground because it causes the lead leg to contact the ground an instant sooner. Even though pressing your hips forward does shorten your stride a little, it still lets you move your legs at maximum speed. Lowering your hands helps control the height your shoulders might rise as you vigorously pump your arms. If arm action is too vigorous and uncontrolled, it will waste energy and could help pull you up and off the ground during high-speed race walking.

Keeping Knees Straight

Bent knees are much easier to detect than loss of contact. Bent-knee competitors look like they are shuffling or creeping on one or both legs, or even jogging. They are getting an extra, unfair push from the large running muscles on the front of their thighs. "Creepers" are usually able to display

A happy 60-plus-year-old glides along, providing enjoyment to herself and all who watch her.

good contact if they don't try to go too fast. Creeping is not a very technical-sounding term, but it does give a good description of what the person is doing.

For many years it was legal for competitive race walkers to land on a slightly bent leg. This knee action was a bit tricky to master, but would aid in thrusting the walker forward if done correctly. A 1995 rule revision requires the advancing

This senior athlete has trained himself to race with the kind of knee action the judges like to see.

leg to be straight, not bent at the knee, when the foot touches the ground. The leg must remain straight all the way back to where it passes directly underneath you, in the vertical upright position, during each step. Only when your leg is at or has passed the vertical upright position is it allowed to be bent at the knee.

Some long-distance (30- to 50-kilometers) race walkers like to land on a slightly bent knee when training because it's easier on their knee joints. Using the large, strong muscles on the front of the thighs to push and thrust the body forward is not what race walking is all about. It must look like walking, not some form of smooth, straightlegged running or semi-jogging.

Incorrect knee action will quickly get you into trouble with the judges because it's so easy to see. Bent-knee walking is a major fault of a fair number of older walkers, especially men. It's the gaining of forward propulsion from bent-knee pushing that makes anyone using this illegal style of race walking look like they are almost or actually running. Race walking must always look like walking.

Once the knee passes the critical vertical position, it must not be quickly bent and used to help thrust the walker forward. Such a move is easily spotted by the judges. To look really good to the judges, and everyone else, the knee of the supporting leg should remain straight an instant longer as it is pulled in and braced back past the vertical upright position.

If done vigorously enough, bent-knee pushing can thrust walkers up, off, and over the ground so that in addition to creeping, they will also be breaking contact with the ground. Bent-knee action can also be used to gain extra stride length and relieve a lot of the strain that correct technique puts on knee joints and hamstring muscles. When the illegal techniques of creeping and lifting are combined, fit walkers will be able to move along at a rapid pace.

Judges should pay more attention to the walker's knee closest to them because of the unobstructed view they have of it. If the leg farther from a judge is questionable, the judge may need to take a position on the other side of the walker for a better view of it the next time the walker passes by. Walkers sometimes have more trouble straightening one leg; judges need to spot that bad leg early and watch its action closely.

Slender legs with large kneecaps have been known to make novice judges think the race walker was walking with a slightly bent knee. All judges need to look closely at the various structures of the walkers' legs to make sure the size of the knee joint is not influencing their decisions. Focusing on the back edge of the knee joint as it passes by sometimes helps provide the clearest picture of how well the knee is straightening.

If you're using too long a stride, this may cause you to restrict your hip rolling and land with bent knees. Some beginners may need to learn how to

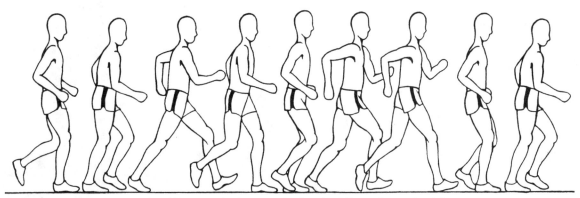

The advancing leg may not land bent at the knee, as in the third figure from the right .
It must land straight, and stay straight, all the way back to the vertical upright position.

It's good to have lots of hope because it helps keep you motivated. Rely on your hope for the persistence and effort needed to achieve future goals. I wish you a lifetime of vigorous, joyful walking.

walk fast by intentionally using shorter steps. Shorter steps will promote the kind of hip and knee action needed to produce faster, more efficient leg speed and better leg straightening and ground contact.

If you have tight hips joints or little hip rotation, you need extra flexibility work. A good exercise for both knees and hips is the fast-walking-in-place drill in chapter 3. Overdoing the hip turning as you walk in place or are training is the best way to loosen up tight hips.

Proper hip and knee action does need to be mastered if you plan on entering future race-walking competitions. Races provide great workouts, opportunities to meet people, travel, and the chance to win a nice award now and then. Make sure your style is legal before entering any race. Mastering and maintaining legal style must always be of primary importance.

I hope you use legal race walking to get healthy and to stay that way and that we meet at a race one of these days.

A Race-walking Photo Scrapbook

5

Competitive race walking has a long and colorful history. The photos on the following pages offer a glimpse of some of the athletes and events from around the world that have shaped the sport over the years. The photos also provide excellent examples of style and technique.

Solid technique being well displayed through the streets of Naples, Italy in 1936.

Henry Laskau, three-time Olympian and outstanding U.S. race walker from 1947 to 1957.

Moscow, July 1958. The author (left) competes in the 20-km race in the USA-USSR meet. The Soviets finished nearly two miles ahead of him that day. It would be fifteen years before Laird finally beat the best Soviet walkers in a major international competition—a lesson in perseverance for anyone!

Colin Young of England during a 24-hour track race.

Madison Square Garden, Feb. 1963. Capt. Ron Zinn winning the national one-mile-walk championship. Captain Zinn was a U.S.A. 20-km walk Olympian in 1960 and 1964. He was killed in action in Vietnam in 1965. Race walking's top performance awards are named in his memory.

Los Angeles Sports Arena, 1964. The start of an indoor one-mile walking race. Look at those heels digging in to pull the ground (a wooden track) back.

San Diego, Calif., June 1965. Start of the national 2-mile championship race.

Northern Poland, 1965. Early going in a 20-km race. We first did a mile on a track, then walked over country roads to another town. The lovely crystal vase that I won is now on display at the Track & Field Hall of Fame in Indianapolis, Indiana.

Start of the 1965 U.S.A. vs U.S.S.R. 20-km walk.
This race started and finished on the stadium
track. The majority of it took place in the streets
of what is now Kiev, Ukraine.

Santa Monica, Calif., 1966. From left, Larry Young,
Ron Laird, and Norm Read compete in a 10-km race.

San Diego, Calif., Feb. 1966. The author on a 100-lap
(25-mile) attempt to break some American long-
distance records. A contest this long is always a
grand test of strength, especially on a warm day. It
is vitally important to stay strong and flexible over
the second half of whatever distance you race.

Good leg, hip, and arm action gets this 1966 Southern California competition quickly off the starting line.

Robert R. Bowman, (right) former chairman of the International Amateur Athletics Federation Walking Committee, competing in a one-hour race in 1966 in San Diego.

Madison Square Garden, 1968. These walkers exhibit good leg-straightening during the New York Athletic Club Games one-mile race. Ron Laird (left) won the event in 6:22.

Pomona, Calif., 1969. Start of the National 20-km Championship.

Larry Walker (left) chases Ron Laird in a one-mile indoor race in Los Angeles in 1973. This distance is the shortest in race walking and demands the utmost concentration and efficiency.

Larry Young of Columbia, Missouri, on his way to third place in the 50-km walk in the 1972 Olympics in Munich, the best performance yet by an American racewalker in international competition.

Hanover, West Germany, 1979. Start of the World Veterans 20-km Championship. Walkers from 40 to over 90 years of age took part in this biennial event. The man out front is the starter.

1984 Olympic 20-km champion, Ernesto Canto of Mexico (left).

1989 World Veterans' Athletics Championships, Eugene, Oregon. Viisha Sedlak (U.S.A.) and Heather McDonald (Australia) display superior knee action during their 10-km event.

1992 Olympic 10-km walk champion Yue Ling Chen of China during a workout. Yue Ling became a U.S citizen in the spring of 2000.

Atlanta, Georgia, 1996. Very fast walking during the Olympic Games 20-km race. Look at all the excellent straight-leg action.

Atlanta, 1996. Olympic Trials 20-km walk.

Master walker Victoria Herazo (age 37) was able to qualify for the 1996 Olympic Games in Atlanta, Georgia.

A young woman's walking race at the 1999 Amateur Athletic Union Junior Olympic Games in Cleveland, Ohio. (See the Resources section for information on the AAU.)

Resources

You can subscribe to or order good fitness and fast-walking material from Elaine Ward, North American Racewalking Foundation, P.O. Box 50312, Pasadena, CA 91115-0312.

Telephone: (626) 441-5459
E-mail: NARWF@aol.com
Website: members.aol.com/RWNARF

Jeff Salvage and Gary Westerfield share over forty years of coaching, racing, and teaching experience in their book, *Walk like an Athlete*. It and two videos can be ordered from Walking Promotions, 79 Lakeside Drive, Medford, NJ 08055.

Telephone: (888) WALK123
Website: www.racewalk.com

Bonnie Stein's AceWalker program has taught race walking to beginners all over the United States. Her classes, camps, and book instruct and motivate people to get fit and stay fit. Contact Bonnie at 209 E. 176 Ave., Redington Shores, FL 33708.

Telephone: (727) 394-WALK
E-mail: AceWalkR@mindspring.com

The staff of the American Walking Association, headed by world masters champion Viisha Sedlak, trains race walkers and coaches, and conducts camps and clinics all over America. American Walking Association, Box 20491, Boulder, CO 80308-3491.

Telephone: (303) 938-9531
E-mail: viisha@viisha.com
Website: www.viisha.com

Coach Howard "Jake" Jacobson has been competing in and teaching health walking and race walking since the late 1960s. His camps, clinics, and books have helped many to get fit and stay fit over the years. Jake Jacobson, Box 640, Levittown, NY 11756.

Website: www.healthwalk.com

Walking and *Prevention* are two good magazines full of health information. Both can be bought at newsstands. You can get current information on fitness walking, nutrition, footwear, clothes, and places to visit for great walks at the *Walking* website.

Website: www.walkingmag.com

Prevention has a walking club with a bimonthly newsletter full of helpful material and encouragement. Write to Prevention Walking Club, Prevention Magazine, 33 E. Minor St., Emmaus, PA 18098.

The Website Racewalker's Link List gives you access to websites worldwide of interest to race walkers. This includes Racewalking 101, an introduction to race walking using animation.

Website: members.aol.com/RWLinkList

Two videos, one for fitness walkers and one for competitors, are available from Martin Rudow at Technique Productions, 4831 N.E. 44th St., Seattle, WA 98105. Martin has over thirty years of experience as a competitor, coach, teacher, and judge.

Telephone: (800) WALKMAX

Dave McGovern, one of America's best competitive race walkers for over a decade has been leading clinics all over North America since 1991. His 1998 book, *The Complete Guide to Racewalking Technique and Training*, and his 2000 book, *The Complete Guide to Walking a Marathon,* can be ordered for $17.95 each, plus $2 for shipping and handling from 43 W. Hathaway Rd., Mobile, AL 36608. Other fitness walking info can be had from Dave's website.

E-mail: RayZwocker@aol.com
Website: surf.to/worldclass

The national magazine for the competitive side of race walking is the *Ohio Racewalker.* In it you will find various articles on the sport, results of races, and a list of future events. The magazine has been edited by 1964 Olympian Jack Mortland since 1965. A subscription is $10 per year (twelve issues) from 3184 Summit St., Columbus, OH 43202.

Bob Carlson, author of *Walking for Health, Fitness, and Sport,* writes a newsletter full of race-walking, fitness, and nutritional information. Contact him at 2261 Glencoe St., Denver, CO 80207.
Telephone: (303) 377-0576

Cheri Korstvedt teaches fitness walking and race walking in the Washington, D.C. and Dallas. Texas areas and gives inspiring motivational lectures.
E-mail: Cheriwalk@aol.com
Website: www.shapewalk.com

The Amateur Athletic Union is a multisport organization dedicated to the promotion and development of amateur sports and physical fitness programs. Most of its athletic competitions are for young (8 to 18) men and women in eight different age groups. The AAU is located in Walt Disney World Resort, P.O. Box 10,000, Lake Buena Vista, Florida 32830.
Telephone: (800) AAU-4USA or (407) 934-7200
Website: www.aausport.org

About the Author

Ronald O. Laird's accomplishments in race walking:

- 4 U.S. Olympic teams, 1960, 1964, 1968, and 1976

- 2 Pan-American Games, 1963 and 1967— Gold Medal at 20 kilometers (12.4 miles), 1967

- 16 other U.S. international teams, 1958–76

- 65 U.S. National Championship wins from 1 mile to 50 kilometers (31.1 miles)

- 4 Canadian National Championship wins

- 53 National Team Championships (three-man) at distances of 10 to 50 kilometers

- 81 U.S. records at distances from 1 kilometer to 25 miles, 1962–76

- Third place in World Cup in 1967 and 1973 at 20 kilometers

- Runner-up Sullivan Award (Outstanding Amateur Athlete), 1970

- 18 All-American men's track and field teams at distances of 1 mile to 50 kilometers, 1958–76

- Outstanding U.S. Race Walker Award, 1963, 1965, 1967, 1969, 1973, and 1976

- Silver medal (20 kilometers) and bronze medal (10 kilometers) in 1979 World Masters Track and Field Championships

- Featured in *Sports Illustrated,* May 8, 1978

- National race-walking coach, 1981–84, Olympic Training Center, Colorado Springs, Colorado

- Inducted into U.S. Track and Field Hall of Fame, December 1986. First race walker so honored.

- Inducted into New York Athletic Club Hall of Fame, December 1992

- The total of sixty-nine U.S. and Canadian titles is the most national championships ever won by any athlete, amateur or professional, in the sport of race walking. This fact has been verified by the *Guinness Book of World Records*

PHOTO CREDITS

Page vi, 31 .... Don Laird

Page viii .... Don Sihler

Page ix, x, 61 (left) .... Beverly LaVeck

Page xi, 5, 6, 7, 9, 24,
    29, 53, 56 (right), 58, 63
    69 (bottom left), 70 (top),
    71 (bottom), 72 (left) .... Tom Carroll

Page 12, 19, 51, 52,
    67 (top), 68 (top),
    69 (top left), 71 (top) .... Eli Attar

Page 20 .... Bonnie Stein

Page 23 .... Richard Horton

Page 26, 73 (bottom left) .... Sportsfoto by
                                    John Allen

Page 32 .... Jeannie Bocci

Page 48 .... Jack Mortland

Page 49 .... Bob Peters

Page 55, 75 (both) .... James Hanley

Page 56 (left) .... Barbara Bules

Page 74 (top) .... Derek Boosey

Page 74 (bottom), 76 .... Jim Janos

Index